County

and the

Surrounding Scenery,

Seat, Families, Etc.

by Mary Jones

First published 1852
Revised and corrected edition published 1875.
This reprint of the 1852 publication by Orchard Publications, 2003.

ORCHARD PUBLICATIONS
2 Orchard Close, Chudleigh, Devon TQ13 0LR
Telephone: (01626) 852714
ISBN 1 898964 59 9

Printed by
Hedgerow Print, Crediton, Devon EX17 1ES

PUBLISHER'S NOTE

The History of Chudleigh by Mary Jones was first published in 1852. A revised and corrected edition followed in 1875 with a preface by the author in which she wrote "To Mr. W. W. Snell I am greatly indebted for his unwearied and disinterested kindness in revising and rearranging the work, as well as examining and correcting proofs".

The variations are several, for example Mary Jones writes about 'Chiderlai' being mentioned in the 1086 Doomsday Book, whereas Snell contradicts this saying the 'Chiderlai' or Manor of Chederleigh mentioned is the one in the parish of Bickleigh, near Tiverton.

The presentation of the second edition also differs from the first or as Mary Jones mentions in the afore-mentioned preface, rearranged.

Whilst recognising these variations and changes we felt it right to reprint the first edition. We have made a few paragraph changes and in places transferred some of the 'old English' into a format more acceptable to today's reader. However the editing we feel is minimal.

Mary Jones was born in Chudleigh in 1797. Her parents were successful in several business enterprises for that period; her father being the sole owner of ships trading local ball clay to continental ports as well as supplying the home markets. Upon her father's death Mary continued to run the business and operated a glass and china warehouse, which as Anthony Crockett in his book 'The Fire of Chudleigh' states, was very probably the Big Jug in Fore Street.

She was much involved in local affairs and was described in the local press as a 'remarkable person' upon her death in 1883 aged 86. When she died she was living in West End, known today as Western House in Fore street.

Chudleigh, July 2003

PREFACE

In presenting the following pages to the public, the writer has been actuated by no other motive than that of supplying the most correct information in her power with respect to this ancient town which, as yet, is without any continuous records of past events.

At the outset it was her intention to have produced a much smaller book, but by the various documents with which she has been favoured, which necessarily enlisted other materials, the work has been much enlarged.

Fully aware of the difficulty in pleasing all tastes, she has laboured with no small diligence in gaining correct information for the historian; so that if she has failed to please, the work shall not be wanting in substantial matter, whereby it may shadow forth that which may be more fully expatiated on hereafter. She has to present her warm acknowledgments to a few friends who have rendered her valuable assistance and information, kindly undertaking also to revise the proof sheets in their passage through the press.

If in any instance she has omitted to acknowledge the authority used, she hopes it will be attributed to inadvertence, rather than to any design of arrogating to herself the honour due to others; and she has now only to add that wherever she has failed in explaining, or fallen short in any way of her object, it has not been from the want of labour, but inability; and with this conviction, she hopes to meet with the indulgence of both reader and critic.

Chudleigh, June 1852

CONTENTS

HISTORY OF CHUDLEIGH

CHAPTER I

The lovely vale which we are about to describe was probably much frequented by the Britons in their wanderings from place to place. They invariably preferred the woods to the plains. Here they could in summer enjoy the cooling shade of its beautiful trees, and in winter the warm shelter of its rocky dells. The chase in which they were so active could not but have been successful and well supplied them with game; and the thickly clothed woods must have also yielded an abundance of nuts, acorns and wild fruits.

Beneath the gloom of the majestic oak that overhung the unbroken and extensive summits of the numerous lime rocks could the Druids by their mysterious rites awe the rude aborigines into subjection. Drewsteignton was the nearest seat of Druidism; as it included a circuit of twenty miles our vale was of course within its limits. It is true that we search in vain for any traces of military works or British fortresses here as are found in other parts of the kingdom, or even neighbouring parishes. The fierce wars in which the Britons often assailed one another, or resisted the common foe, appear to have been carried on altogether beyond its precincts, and imagination pictures these restless tribes having here a safe retreat, a kind of happy valley, to which they could occasionally resort, lying between the wilds of Dartmoor and the dangers incident to a dwelling on the southern coast, which was often attacked by fierce and successful invaders, especially the Belgae.

The Romans who subdued Britain under the Caesars passed over their own highway that lay considerably east of the town. Although they had a beacon on Haldon, and another at Hazlewood (that leads west from Hennock village), yet they have left us no remains that prove their ever having had a station within this vale. Compelled by wars near home the Romans gradually withdrew their forces from the island, and finally quitted it about the middle of the fifth century. It may be worthy a passing notice as showing the high estimation in which the Romans held the Britons, that they took with them to the seat of empire many young British soldiers whom they had studiously trained to war.

Julius Caesar on his first landing readily distinguished the native Britons as a race altogether superior in stature and beauty to the Gauls or Belgae, whom he then found in possession of our coasts.

> *"Rude as the wilds, around his sylvan home,*
> *In savage grandeur, see the Briton roam:*
> *Bare were his limbs, and strung with toil and cold,*
> *By untam'd nature cast in giant mould:*
> *O'er his broad brawny shoulders loosely flung,*
> *Shaggy and long, his yellow ringlets hung."*

The Britons as soon as freed from the dominion of the Romans, were assailed by the Picts and Scots. Wanting aid in these defensive wars, they most unwittingly craved the assistance of some barbarous tribes that dwelt on the shores of the German Ocean whom we now include under the general name of Saxons. These tribes after aiding the Britons, like many other public and private benefactors, took good care to serve themselves by retaining possession of the island. They cruelly oppressed the noble Britons and massacred all whom they found openly professing Christianity. Gregory, justly surnamed the Great, mourned for the sufferings of the infant church, then gradually (from the holy lives of its ministers and professors) advancing in public estimation, sent Augustine and other pious missionaries to Britain in 597 to convert if possible these barbarous and iniquitous usurpers to the faith of Christianity. They were kindly received and their interesting mission proved most successful.

The Saxons, as is well known, divided the kingdom into seven independent states and then quarrelled among themselves. Under Ceadwalla, King of Wessex, one of the most powerful of these Saxon princes, whose reign commenced about 685, we may conclude that our town began to be formed, and from him according to Polwhele, some have supposed it derived its Saxon name of Chidley, although the same historian further says that others thought that Chudleigh may have been derived from 'cid', contention and 'ley', a lock; another from 'cud', a hiding and 'leigh', place, thus signifying a hiding place. The Saxons had in their turn to bear the horrors of invasion.

The Danes possessed the empire of the sea, were continually ravaging the coasts of Britian, and first landed at Teignmouth about the year 800. The attention of the reader has to be directed to the Danish encampment in the heights of Ugbrooke Park. This was probably occupied by the Danes about the year 876, as at that time they overran the southern part of the county. During the occupation of this camp, whether many or few, the inhabitants of our vale were no doubt compelled to hide themselves, or escape for their lives towards the moorlands.

It was at this period, according to Lysons, that Exeter fell into the hands of these marauders, and were there besieged by Alfred and compelled by that good and great king to surrender, leaving him such hostages as he demanded. The rude Saxon under him, one of the best monarchs that ever swayed a sceptre, began from this period rapidly to emerge from comparative barbarism into civilisation. The Christian religion was cordially embraced; parishes and even mother churches were known as early as 907, in the reign of Edgar. Chudleigh, with the other towns of Devonshire, now began rapidly to advance into importance, the bounds of the parish were without doubt established, a Christian community instituted, and a place of worship erected. Dr. Oliver supposes the parish church to have preceded the palace; it must not of course be understood that the early structure was in extent, or importance, to be compared to the church afterwards dedicated to St. Martin in 1259, by Bishop Bronscombe. The site might have been the same, but the building doubtless differed essentially, and had then either to be enlarged or re-erected, and again consecrated.

In the Doomsday-book (which contained a general survey of the island, begun 1081 and completed 1086 by William the Conqueror) Chudleigh is entered as Chiderleia, the land of the Earl of Moreton, so say Polwhele and Lysons in their histories of Devon. Order was again quickly restored after the Norman conquest; under new leases the land in many instances remained in the possession of its original occupiers. In the eleventh and twelfth centuries the Roman Catholic Church rapidly extended its ecclesiastical domination throughout the length and breadth of the land. Bishop Leofric, in 1050, removed the See from Crediton to Exeter and, with the latter, Chudleigh soon became intimately associated. One of the early bishops, about the year 1080, attracted by the salubrity of the air and the beauty of the vale, selected it and Paignton as sites for his rural palaces. Others were afterwards erected at Bishopsteignton, Tawton, etc. The vale of Chudleigh was without baronial castle or other secular domain of importance. The bishops of Exeter may therefore be considered to have been, from the conquest to the Reformation, the undisputed lords, temporal, as well as spiritual, of this district, having everything that concerned its welfare under their entire control. The Chudleigh palace was without doubt a favourite residence of the early bishops. In a chapel attached to it and dedicated to St. Michael, there were frequent ordinations; many documents now in the archives of Exeter Cathedral were signed when these prelates sojourned in this rural retreat. Dr. Oliver, in his ecclesiastical history of Devon, mentions the appropriation of the park, manor, and valuable lands to the See of Exeter, as shown by a deed between 1161 and 1184, wherein Bishop Bartholomew grants the profit of his woods in Chudleigh to the Leper-house of St. Magdalen in Exeter. He tells us also that in 1282 the manor of Chudleigh was annexed to the precentorship of Exeter Cathedral by Bishop Quivil.

In the register of Bishop Stapledon in 1308, we find the rental of the manor to be £17 4s. 5¼d. About this time the woollen trade (noticed elsewhere) was carried on extensively and the fulling mill paid twenty shillings per annum to the See of Exeter. For the collection of rents and other business connected with the manor the precentor was, by the liberality of the bishops, provided with a house and certain lands at Ugbrooke. And in the will of Hugh de Hyckeling, then precentor, dated the 8th August, 1415 and proved 1416, there is a bequest of money and of his livestock at Ugbrooke.

It was optional for the Bishop of Exeter to receive from the manor of Chudleigh at Christmas either twenty-four woodcocks or twelvepence. Bishop Stapledon, with a view of increasing the prosperity of the town of Chudleigh (then rapidly advancing) procured for it in 1309 from his sovereign, Edward II, a charter for the market and fairs. Among the lands which this bishop purchased, for the maintenance of his obit (or masses for his soul) as stated in his ordinance dated 2nd March, 1321, these were enumerated some as being situated at Waddene, in this parish. Edward Pyry was keeper of the park and bailiff to Bishop Lacy. In 1447 he was appointed with a salary of twelvepence per week.[1] - thus far Dr. Oliver.

The venerable prelate as the Dr. styles Bishop Lacy, after governing the church thirty-five years, died at the Chudleigh palace in 1455, and was interred in Exeter Cathedral. His arms were set up in the east wall of the north aisle of Chudleigh church. This bishop was highly esteemed for his sanctity: 'there was a great resort of pilgrims to his tomb, at which many miracles were pretended to have been performed'. It may be worth notice that this bishop entertained Henry VI, in 1451, for eight days, at his palace in Exeter, the charges being borne equally by the church and city. From Bishop Lacy, to the instalment of Veysey, there is comprised a period of sixty eight years. A list of the successive Roman Catholic bishops is the only link presenting itself by which the chain of events can be continued. These bishops (it will be seen) were sadly departing from their original simplicity and sanctity. They were frequently translated from one See to another, were close attendants on royalty, as well as deeply involved in politics and secular affairs.

Bishop Lacy was succeeded by George Neville in 1455, who was installed at the age of nineteen and made Lord Chancellor of England at twenty-five, in the reign of Henry VI.

John Booth succeeded Neville and was consecrated in 1466; but weary of the turmoil in which the bishops were ever involved at this disturbed period of our history, he returned to his own mansion in Hampshire where he died.[2]

Peter Courtenay was consecrated bishop in 1479; he was son of Sir Philip Courtenay of Powderham, was in great favour with Henry VII, and was translated to Winchester.

Richard Fox was next installed Bishop of Exeter in 1486; he was the faithful counsellor of Henry VII. This bishop was one of the most shrewd and wise men of his day, and had the honour of being godfather to the king's second son, afterwards Henry VIII. Oliver

King was made bishop in 1492. Richard Redmayn was translated from Wales to Exeter in 1495, and from thence to Ely. John Arundell, descended from a Cornish family, was installed in the See of Exeter in 1504. Hugh Oldham[3] was preferred to Exeter in 1507; he was involved for years in a dispute with the abbot of Tavistock. While this lawsuit was pending he died, and being then under sentence of excommunication at Rome, he could not be interred, until absolution was procured. It does not appear from any existing records that these bishops, who had most of them become the restless votaries of ambition, showed any partiality for the palace at Chudleigh, or interest in the welfare of the town; and John Veysey, who was the successor of Hugh Oldham, had so little regard for that which belonged to the See of Exeter that he not only abandoned, but absolutely alienated the manor and demesne. This prelate was promoted to the bishoprick of Exeter in 1523. He was in great favour with Henry VIII, was made Lord President of Wales, and was godfather to the king's eldest daughter, The Lady Mary, and to his government was this princess afterwards committed.

Troublous times now approached the English Roman Catholic Church, its greatest foes were within its own pale; important results followed the downfall of this long established hierarchy, and the termination of its ecclesiastical domination throughout England. In these events our little town, as may be implied from its past history, was deeply interested; an entire new order of circumstances followed, which will form the subject of the following chapter.

1. The best quality of wheat was sold in Exeter Market at 6d. per bushel, about this period.

2. Bishop Booth, says Izacke, built the stately chair in the choir of his church; being finished he could not quietly sit down therein, so troublesome were the times by reason of the civil wars between the houses of York and Lancaster.

3. Bishop Oldham founded the Free Grammar School of Manchester in 1519, which seems to have been the year of his death.

CHAPTER II

The glorious cause of the Reformation was but disgraced, as coupled with a name so odious as that of Henry VIII,[1] he is only here noticed as the friend and patron of Veysey, and like him, engaged in the work of spoliation.

While Henry, by the strong arm of arbitrary power, stripped most of the religious houses belonging to the Roman Catholics throughout England of the treasures they had been accumulating and guarding for centuries, Veysey was quietly doing the same with the rural palaces in Devon, and selling or leasing all the valuable ecclesiastical property committed to his charge. He might it is true (from the signs of the times) have felt convinced that what he thus squandered would be likely soon to pass into other hands, but this could furnish no reasonable excuse for his careless expenditure, neither had he any right to gratify his ambition in the enlargement of the place of his nativity (Sutton Coldfield, Warwickshire) at the cost of the church over which he was called to preside as one "that had to give an account of his stewardship". He is described by an old writer "*as having been thro' the whole course of his life, courtlike and bountiful, which in the end tended not so much to his credit, as the spoil of the church, for of twenty-two manors, or lordships, which his predecessors had enjoyed (and left to him of a great yearly revenue) he left but three to his successors, and those also leased out; and where he found fourteen mansion houses excellently well furnished, he left but one, and that very bare and naked*". The proceedings of Bishop Veysey in the alienation of the church lands in this parish principally concern our history, and they are thus recorded.

In the first year of the reign of Edward VI and on the 6th February, he granted a lease for ninety-nine years of the manor, town of

Chudleigh, park, palace and lime-kiln, commonly called Chudleigh calce, to the Duke of Somerset; and in the third year of the same reign he was licensed to alienate the manor of Chudleigh in favour of Thomas Bridges, Esquire of Tangley in Oxfordshire. At this period, and long after, there appears to have been continued changes in connection with the holding of manorial rights and valuable lands, occasioned by the alienation of church property; at least, such was the case in Devon; many speculations were afloat in buying, selling and leasing the same.

The Duke of Somerset does not appear to be afterwards mentioned in reference to the property that was thus leased to him, as about this time the park must have been alienated to Sir Peter Courtenay,[2] "whose daughter and co-heiress, brought it to Anthony Clifford of Borscombe, in Wilts. and Kingsteignton in Devon". Lawell, another portion of the church property, passed into the hands of Eastchurch, and his name is coupled with that of Mr. Clifford in the management of the local affairs of the parish soon after the Reformation. The manor of Chudleigh, which we have just stated to have been purchased by Thomas Bridges, was again sold by him, or probably by a son of the same name, in 1589, to Thomas Hunt of Hams Barton in this parish, and John Hunt resold it to Hugh Lord Clifford for the sum of £253 7s. 0d. and by this family it is still possessed. It may also be worthy of notice, although shown elsewhere, that Hams, belonging to the Waddon district, was an ancient inheritance, forming no part of the church property. Although the pedigree of the Hunts is not traced farther back than 1500, the old mansion house must have been built long before. No records exist concerning it of an earlier date as the Hunts originally belonged to Exeter and they no doubt obtained this inheritance by purchase.

After the death of Henry VIII, from the alteration of religion, "a rebellion that broke out in this diocese was imputed partly to Bishop Veysey, because he lay far from it and dwelt in his own country; whereupon he resigned the bishoprick into the hands of Edward VI" when it was presented to Miles Coverdale, a reformed monk, born in Yorkshire, who was consecrated at Lambeth in 1551 to the See of Exeter by Thomas Cranmer. It is indeed an interesting fact that this learned and excellent man was the first Protestant bishop of our county. He spent his time in translating the scriptures into the vernacular tongue and, to prevent being interrupted in his great work, committed the whole charge of his ecclesiastical jurisdiction to an able and excellent co-adjutor, Robert Weston, who was afterwards Lord Chancellor of Ireland.

The death of the youthful and pious Edward changed the tide of affairs and they were destined again to roll back on superstition, bigotry and oppression. By the accession of Mary the Reformation was suspended and the Roman Catholic religion re-established. Coverdale was ejected from the See of Exeter and compelled to fly to the King of Denmark for protection. John Veysey, the lavish squanderer of the revenues of the church, was again Bishop of Exeter.

During this eventful period of our history, when the fierce persecutions of Mary's days were raging, the fires of Smithfield reached us not; the martyrdom of the faithful was chiefly confined to London, Norfolk, Essex and Kent. However, the terrible blast swept through the length and breadth of the land, if not in its reality, yet in terror and amazement. They were indeed days of mourning and lamentation to all but the cruel persecutors themselves.

Soon after the accession of Elizabeth, Coverdale was again offered the See of Exeter, but preferred ending his days in comparative obscurity. He died in London, May 20th, 1567.

The sale of the manor and church lands by Veysey terminated the long established domination of the Catholics in Chudleigh, and the Reformation entirely swept away the profession of its faith from this town and neighbourhood; there is no tradition or record whatever of its having been retained. Its introduction took place more than a century after this period by the Lord Treasurer Clifford, who embraced the Catholic faith in the days of Charles II. His ancestors during the interval, from the Reformation to the time of the Lord Treasurer, had been zealous Protestants, and deeply interested in the welfare of the established church. The Chapel at Ugbrooke was built by him, and consecrated by Bishop Sparrow.[3]

All that fell to the parish of Chudleigh, in the general confusion at the Reformation, were a few inconsiderable church lands, not particularised in Bishop Veysey's leases. The fairs and markets, procured for the town by Bishop Stapledon, appear to have been in the possession of Hunt, and were redeemed by the parish for a trifling amount; these became the principal source of parish revenue. The advowson or the vicarage of the parish church, soon after became the property of Hunt and, as will be shown in connection with a description of the church, was sold by Thomas Hunt to the parishioners in 1685. The rectory or great tithes belonged to the See of Exeter some time after the Reformation, for we read *"that the perpetuity of the rectory of Chudleigh was granted to the Lord Treasurer Clifford and his heirs male, and heirs general, by Charles II, on the 4th April, 1673, but with the obligation of paying the sum of £42 per annum to the precentor of Exeter Cathedral"*. This was a heavy rental, according to the value of money in those days; the great tithes are now commuted at £255 per annum. From the period of the reformation there was in Chudleigh, as throughout the rural districts generally, a blending of civil and ecclesiastical institutions.

The vestry of the church became the grand arena for all discussions concerning the temporal, as well as spiritual, prosperity of the inhabitants. The parish chest (still in the vestry) was the public treasury. The belfry was the weekly relieving office, and the church tower was occupied with stores which were frequently sold therefrom for the benefit of the parish.

The register book of baptisms, marriages and burials commences about the first year of the reign of Elizabeth, and afterwards appears to have been corrected throughout by the Rev. R.Woolcombe, the vicar of Chudleigh, in 1600. About this time an entry is made in the parochial register of *"two shillings pd. to Nics. Thorne for wryting eight leaves in the new pchmt. booke"*. The account book or parochial registers also commence with the reign of Elizabeth, and these show that the parish was managed by a body of men annually chosen by the parishioners in vestry. They consisted of seven and were always designated 'the seven men'. Four of these seven appear to have acted in the capacity of treasurers of the parish funds; two were called 'high store wardens', and two 'the young men's wardens'. The various meetings and consultations of these worthies, and the principal inhabitants in the said vestry, were no doubt frequently most interesting, but of the various entries made by order of 'the seven men', in the records handed down to posterity, the greater part relate to pounds shillings and pence.

The usual summary method of punishment which they adopted were shipping and setting unhappy culprits in the stocks, unruly females on the cucking stool,[4] and ejecting itinerant beggars in a barrow to the next tithing. 'The seven men' were evidently no greater scribes than their neighbours, for the first entry in these records in 1558 is an item, a clerk was *"pyde for wrytting of this count, iiiid"*. The principal source of revenue, as just stated, were the tolls of the fairs and markets. In 1561 they yielded an income of £11 6s. 10d.

13

These continued gradually to advance until 1614, when they were let for five years for £100. In 1626 the town was visited by a contagious disorder, which was designated a plague, and an allowance in consequence of the loss sustained by the absence of the usual frequenters of the market was made to the renter of the tolls, ending the 20th April, 1627. There was also provision made in consequence of this and other calamities, which had from time to time visited the town, in the future letting of the fairs and markets; for in 1651 the rent was £67 per annum "provided there were no contagious sickness, fire or visible loss by means of soldiers, or other considerations, shall be had thereof, reasonable allowance given". The rent of the fairs and markets still advanced, for in 1677 they amounted to the sum of £120 per annum.

It had been the custom of 'the seven men' to provide an annual dinner on the market account day, and for the use of these banquets, in 1577, we find item *"paide for six dozen tranchers"*. These dinners were discontinued in 1609 and an entry to this effect *"that there shall be no dinner hereafter provided at the market account day, at the charge of the parish".*[5] All that could be saved was treasured up by 'the seven men' for the benefit of the parish.[6] The year before this economical movement a proposition was made by Mr. Clifford to begin the building of alms houses with the cash then in hand.

It was the custom of 'the seven men' to lend small sums to the poor gratis, upon bills to be taken of their sureties for them, and to be returned on the next annual market account 'daie', as appears in an item *"that the use of the parsons of Chudleigh's monie ten pounds six shillings, should be yearly distributed among the poor of the parish upon 'Whitson daie', and that two persons shall be appointed for the setting out of the amount, to be lent to the poor"*. Money made a high rate of interest in 1598 for the use of ten pounds, borrowed for the parish, twenty shillings interest per annum was paid.

The building of the alms houses was carried into effect in 1611, under the superintendence of Mr. Hugh Clifford. Various sums entered for their erection were a kind of floating capital until their completion. These alms houses were evidently much needed, there being some troublesome poor; this was manifested by an order the same year that *"Beaton Bucketmaker and her companie, shall be removed out of the church porch chamber upon the next visitation of my Lord Bishop or before Barnabus daie next"* and that *"that chamber shall be no more sett to time without consent of Mr. Clifford, Mr. Eastchurch, Mr. Putt, the vicar and others of the chiefest inhabitants of the parish"*. The letting of the western church porch chamber was suspended henceforth and the then sexton, William Bailiffe, was to have in lieu of the church porch *"five shillings, to be paid on the general account daie"*.

The organs mentioned in the parish records were no doubt in the rood-loft; they say paid to *"organ players, and also for other commodities for the parish"*, and in 1568 *"for singeing (singing) bread"*, and in 1577 *"item paid for pulling down the rood-loft"*,[7] In 1591 *"for money laid out and in part payment for the organs, and for carriage of them, and divers things bestowed in and about the same, as by bill thereof appeareth"*; in 1605 *"paid for a lock for the organs, and for mending a pipe"*. On May 10th, 1608 *"promised, by Mr. Clifford and Mr. James Eastchurch, that they will mount and erect the organs upon a stage fairly fitted before Christmas next for four pounds, to be paid to them by the market man between this day and the next general account day"*. These two organs had each a single row of pipes, treble and bass, and of course two performers were required to play them in full choir. From 1555 there are entries of several sums as paid to players; these are without doubt the organ players. In 1569, item *"paid to the organ players, sixteen shillings"*.

It is certain there were two instruments: 'organs' is the entry in all these records, in addition to which a perforated oak sound board for a single row of treble pipes was firmly affixed to the belfry screen for a seat; this was evidently a part of one of these instruments.

After the organs fell into disuse, the choir was led by stringed and other instruments. In the north aisle or transept, there were three rising seats traditionally called the tenor, treble and bass seats. From these seats the choir removed to the western gallery when erected, and the original singing seats were occupied as pews.

On a further perusal of the parish records we find that 'the seven men' not only supplied the poor from the belfry, but they literally converted it into a kind of general warehouse and sold the goods that were there collected. These stores appear to have occupied the first floor of the tower, and the first large pew to the right, approaching the church from the belfry, which pew was always called the 'bacon hutch' till the alteration of the church in 1848. The record says item, *"received for bread, and other stuffs[8] which they gathered, one pound four shillings and fourpence; item for alle sold, three pounds nine shillings and fourpence. One thousand five hundred and eighty-nine, received for our bread, and other things sold in the church, one pound six shillings and eightpence; item for the church loffe, eight shillings."*

It is evident that at this period dogs were most numerous and that, finding food was stored in the church, they became very troublesome. All necessary precaution was taken by 'the seven men' to keep them off; consequently a person was hired to be in attendance at certain times for this purpose. In 1591 there is an item, *"paid John Macey for keeping the dogges from the church, sixpence"*; and in 1599, *"paid to Nicholas Bobbish, for one quarter, for whipping out the dogges from the church, tenpence"*. Thus arose without doubt the custom

16

used even at the present day in towns and villages, of styling the verger the 'dogwhipper'.

1. Alison in the Life of John Duke of Marlborough, mentions that Henry VIII brought to the scaffold during his reign seventy-two thousand persons.
2. Sir Peter Courtenay, as stated in *Cliffordiana*, second son of Sir William Courtenay of Powderham, was the first lay possessor of Ugbrooke; he died the 20th May, 1552. Ugbrooke seems to have been the jointure of his widow Elizabeth, but with reversion to her son-in-law Anthony Clifford, who had married her third daughter, Anne.
3. The Bishop of Exeter did accordingly proceed to its consecration, *"per nomen Cemeterii et Capellae S. Cypriani"*, on the 17th July, 1671, and commends Clifford's pious and religious devotion. But it is unquestionably true that he declared himself a Catholic before the commencement of the year 1673." *(Cliffordiana)*
4. This instrument was a sort of chair, placed at the end of a plank, in which the offender was placed and ducked. It was formerly made use of to punish bakers and brewers, upon transgressing the laws made in relation to their several trades; for upon offending in this respect they were ducked or plunged in some stinking or muddy pond by means of this chair. (Gregory's Dict.)
5. The tranchers were no doubt sold to advantage when the annual banquets were suspended.
6. The expense of recreations was still continued and paid for out of the parish funds; there are items, viz: by payment of rent for the bowling green to Mr. Putt at 30s. per annum, and expense of composition for the same, £12; with comfortable seats as appears by an item *"mending the 'skeling stoule' and timber for the same. Writing of the articles for the bowling green."* The barbarous practice of bull baiting also appears to be sanctioned by 'the seven men'; there is an entry for *"mending the bull ring"*.
7. A gallery in the church on which relics or images were set to view.
8. The rates were partly collected in grain, etc.

CHAPTER III

The disturbed state of England during the reigns of Mary and Elizabeth, occasioned by religious dissensions, extended itself to this remote part of the kingdom. Although at that time no regular standing army was kept up, yet we find on referring to the parish records, in 1567 an item paid for *"setting forth of soldgers"*, under the order issued by government to train a certain number to arms throughout the country, seeing there would be required a force of men on account of these disturbances. In 1572 there is an item, *"paid to Michael Bobbish to goe to Exeter to fetch the cutler to clean the parish harness"*; another item in 1575, *"paid for bombaste[1] for the souldiers"*; item, *"paid to the cutler for dressing the armour, and paid the same cutler for two gorgetts"*; in 1578, *"paid to Thomas Cade for training of the soldiers, and to Nichs. Bennett at the home coming of the solders"*; *"more to him for mending a sword and dagger"* (broke in exercise and not in real action); and in 1580, *"paid Greene for stocking of the calliver"* (a small ship's gun), for the county was now in a high state of disorder. *"Paid for seven swords, seven sword girdles and seven daggers."* 1st July, *"paid for two dozen points to tye the parish harness",[2]* these points were strings, used to fasten parts of the dress before that useful invention, buttons. Item, *"paid for two pounds of gunpowder; for drying the same, sixpence"*; this was a small remuneration for so dangerous an undertaking; *"paid for a leather bag to carry the gunpowder, sixpence"*.

In 1585, *"paid to the man that had the commission for Archerie, and also to the men that wore the parish armour at Totnes"*, where there was no doubt a general muster of the military forces of the South Hams, in consequence of the threatened invasion of the Spaniards, which was attempted soon after. Nothing could exceed the terror and consternation which pervaded all classes throughout England, and especially Devon, when the Spanish Armada was announced to be in the English Channel and within sight of Plymouth, where it was however defeated, principally by the gallantry of Drake, a native of the county, born at Tavistock. This signal victory was gained in 1588.

From this period to the termination of the reign of Elizabeth, nothing particular occurred to disturb the peace of the county. Affairs appeared still tranquil during the following reign of James I. The woollen trade was then active; the inhabitants were busily employed in combing, spinning, weaving and fulling: fields on the other side of Kate-brook are still designated the 'tucking fields'. There are no accounts of the number of serges manufactured or of the amount of wages then paid weekly. The only criterion by which any conclusion can be arrived at is the annual rent of the market and fairs, and this was considerable. The parish armour was again held in readiness and examined in 1627, two years after the accession of Charles I, and was then said to consist of ten head pieces and murrions, two bills and one tuck, three callivers, four corsletts, and two muskets, in Mr. Vaughan's[3] custody. From this period the contention between the unfortunate Charles and the parliament continued to increase: the king's obstinacy, and the inflexible spirit of the parliamentarians whose liberties they justly considered the king to have infringed on, broke out into open war and deluged England in bloodshed and confusion.

We read in Lysons, *"that when the civil war commenced in the seventeenth century, the whole of Devon was in the hands of the committees of safety, and the majority of the inhabitants attached to the parliament"*. Whether this be the case or not as it respects this county, it is quite certain that the king's affairs were so managed as in many instances to convert his friends into open foes, for instead of his forces being disciplined and concentrated, they were scattered throughout the kingdom. About 6,000 horse and foot were scouring the west of England. These were idle and dissolute, creating disorder and confusion wherever they came. In many places the inhabitants rose against them. Chudleigh had no alternative but to afford them entertainment. Soldiers were passing to and fro, sometimes remaining quartered on the town for days together. Numerous sums of money had to be paid by 'the seven men', out of the slender resources of the parish funds. There is in the records a particular note of disbursements kept by Abraham Pinsent from which a few items will be given.

Parties of the royalists occupied Chudleigh successively from the summer of 1644 to January, 1646. Item, for *"meate and drink for two troopers, when the Prince's troope quartered here, being the second of September, one thousand six hundred and forty-five; also for Captain Carey and his men, horses and the guarde. Eight seames of fagot and four seames of hard wood when Major General Molesworth was here; for the hay of eight horses, that came with ammunition at the same time, being here three days and three nights. Wood for the guards that watcht ye ammunition when Colonel Sheeley was here two days and two nights. Wood for the guards and for sick men belonging to Colonel Wise's regiment, from the tenth of November to the tenth of December; for Lieutenant Colonel Porter's and divers other commanders of Colonel Sheeley's regiment, and their horses"*. It appears that a dinner had to be provided for Lord Wentworth, at Colonel Wise's quarters, on which occasion there was *"paid for three pullets, one and sixpence"*. To conclude the extracts referring to the visits of the royalists, of which many others could be selected, we find *"paid to the constable in monie ten pounds"*: this sum no doubt included various outlays as well as much time employed in providing for such expensive and troublesome visitors.

Chudleigh shared largely in the general consternation of this eventful period of our history. Besides the heavy expenses the peaceful inhabitants were no doubt in great dread of a collision between the contending parties. From the next entry we find how likely this was to have taken place, *"since ye parliament army cometh hither"*. On their arrival the parish was again taxed with heavy expenses, as we read, from *"the ninth of January one thousand six hundred and forty-six and onwards in different entries, for eight-nine seames of wood for the guards"*; with them are coupled the names of *"Colonel English, Major Finchen, Lieutenant Colonel Herbert, Colonel Sheffield and other officers"*. In addition to the wood, the winter being most severe, there are entries of *"meate and drink for troopers, waggoners, guards, sick and wounded soldiers which were quartered here until March"*. Fairfax lodged in the town one night at least; even Cromwell, having intelligence that a party of the royalists lay at Bovey Tracey, passed with his forces through Trusham and Hennock as the most private route, and there surprised the royalist leaders who were quietly enjoying a game at cards, but they had the presence of mind to throw their stakes out at the window and, while the money was scrambled for by Cromwell's troop, they escaped across the Bovey river.

The success that attended the parliamentarian forces under Cromwell and Fairfax in Devonshire, as elsewhere, is too well known to need comment here. Interesting particulars of the different skirmishes that took place are already before the public. 'Cromwell's troopers', as our records style them, had each to carry a foot soldier behind; when arrived at the scene of action they would present a double invincible force, such as left to the royalists no chance of success, although aided by many of the leading men of the county. Dartmouth was the last port in Devonshire possessed by Charles' forces and there fell one of our influential and wealthy neighbours,

Sir George Chudleigh, whose ancestors are said to have been originally of this town. It is thus related by Lysons, *"Major General Chudleigh was accused of treachery in these civil contentions; however, he was taken prisoner by the royalists when by the kindness of his captors, and the unjust accusations of his own party, he went over to the king's party, and was killed at the siege of Dartmouth"*.

As seen by the local records, Chudleigh was occupied by some of the principal actors in all this civil, or rather uncivil, bloody strife of one party of Englishmen against another. It was also a deposit for ammunition and head quarters for the royalists. Hams Barton is supposed to have been occupied by Colonel Wise, and it is there no doubt that Lord Wentworth was entertained.

The inhabitants acted most wisely in preserving a strict neutrality, receiving each party in turn. Had any strife arisen some account would have been handed down by history or tradition. Before entering on the records relative to the era of the protectorate, it may be observed that Cromwell was inflexible in the pursuit of what he thought right; vigilant and active in the administration of justice, and courageous as a warrior, his greatest enemies have been compelled to acknowledge that all his measures for the welfare of the country were of the highest political order, and crowned with abundant success both at home and abroad. Compelled by his position to keep up a powerful military force, officers of the army were sent through the country to levy both horses and money. Chudleigh did not escape a visit, for we find in the parochial registers that in 1652, *"Mr. Woolcombe's (vicar) mare and saddle and Roger Winsor's ditto, were purchased by 'the seven men' for ten pounds fifteen shillings; there was also paid to the captain, by general consent, two pounds sixteen shillings"*. *"Fire and candles for the troop, three shillings"*. This recruiting party without doubt took the horses to head quarters. Humphrey Pinsent, renting the fairs and markets at this time, was evidently accountant to 'the seven men' and as a deduction hung on the contingency of war, made an entry accordingly; it runs thus: *"allowance which I crave in time of war, one pound ten shillings"*.

Nothing of importance occurred from the termination of the civil war to disturb the tranquility of our town; indeed it seems to have preserved a peaceful character throughout all its generations; even when fierce and bloody contests raged around and beyond, the monster evil of wholesale murder came not once within this lovely vale. Here are no ruins of ivy covered battlements marking where lie the brave and noble; no clarion calling to warfare has ever sent its shrill echoes through our peaceful woods; here is no battlefield 'where the spade, the plough, disturb our ancestors'.

It may be interesting to turn again to the records as developing the anxious and unceasing concern manifested by 'the seven men' and others for the welfare of the parish.

The Rev. Robert Woolcombe, already mentioned in the registers, succeeded his father, Benedict Woolcombe, and was instituted to the vicarage of Chudleigh in 1600; in his latter years, being by age and infirmities unable to discharge the duties of the parish, he was aided by a curate, Charles Wills. 'The seven men' agreed to pay him £10 yearly, 'to be no precedent for the future'. Robert Woolcombe died January 22nd, 1654. After his death the parish was without a vicar, there being several entries at this time of sums paid for occasional supplies.

The civil and religious strife that so long distracted the country had no doubt the effect of thinning the ranks of theological students in the colleges, for instead of there being a host of applicants, not even one came forward to apply for the vacant benefice. At the time of this vacancy the living was at the disposal of William Putt and James and Thomas Eastchurch; they with 'the seven men' convened a meeting. The interesting particulars of the resolutions then passed are well worth being quoted in full: *"Having this day met and conferred together touching the procuring of, and provision to be made for an orthodox and settled minister here in this our parish, have thereupon resolved as follows: Mr. Giles Inglett, one of 'the seven men', be directed forthwith to write away to Oxford to such of his acquaintance as he shall think fitt, for the purpose aforesaid: that when such a man as shall be thought fitt shall be pitcht on; 'the seven men' according to the power to them given doe cause such moneys belonging to the parish as shall be requisite to be paid over and disbursed towards his journey and preparation thereof hither, that after his coming hither, he staying here half a year upon tryall, shall be payed after the rate of eighty pounds, paid out of the tythes of the said parish, and an augmentation out of the fayers and markets; that what charges Mr. Inglett shall be at in entering a caveat above, or any other means in order to the said moneys belonging to the parish, and also for his paynes and trouble in and about the same."* After thus deputing Mr. Giles Inglett to the important office of getting an orthodox minister, 'the seven men' with all diligence *"requested Richard Manley and Humphrey Shapter to enquire after and view the surplisses, organ pipes and seats, and to certify howe they shall find the same at the next meeting of 'the seven men', and that the churchwardens be spoken to, that they take orders for the repairs of the clock, much in decay"*. Mr. Giles Inglett was most successful in his application for a sound orthodox divine for we read another entry to the purport that *"Humphrey Shapter be ordered to pay out of his receipts, unto Mr. Giles Inglett, forty shillings, to discharge a note of disbursements for the parish, amounting to twenty-one shillings, and the residue is a gratitude (gratuity) to him and his son for their paynes and care in procuring Mr. Bloy, as well as for other services"*.

On the 10th May, 1658 the parishioners and 'the seven men' met for the purpose of making arrangements for the new minister, Mr. Bloy, who was come from Oxford on trial; forty shillings was immediately paid towards his journey hither. All necessary repairs as well as the cleansing and renovating the interior of the church were effected before his arrival. 'The seven men' and the influential parishioners again met (none joined these consultations but the wealthy and respectable); they proceeded most judiciously, observing the strictest economy. In October it is further entered that Mr. Bloy is to have besides the vicarage and premises, £20 per annum, to be paid quarterly, and twenty marks towards his procuring the great seal for his induction. There was great anxiety that all necessary preliminaries for his being in full possession should be completed if possible before Easter, as the following entry proves: *"that he (Mr. Bloy) will procure himself ordained a minister before the twenty-fifth day of March, or so soone as convenientlye he canne, and that the payment of the twenty pounds yearly not to commence until he be inducted to the said vicarage and ordained a minister before the twenty-fifth day of March next; then to have ten pounds for that half yeare"*; Mr. Bloy was regularly inducted before Easter. The gown and surplices, after a careful examination, were found altogether the worse for wear and keeping, and an item is accordingly entered *"paid for a new gown, four pounds"*, and the surplices repaired, which in those days were made of dowlas. The worthy vicar, obtained under such interesting circumstances, gave great satisfaction during the fifteen years of his ministerial labours, and at his decease left a donation to the parish of £30.

Charles II ascended the throne under circumstances the most propitious, but he destroyed his own well-being and the prosperity of the nation by profligate extravagance and an inordinate love of pleasure. The interesting fact that one of his prime ministers was born at Ugbrooke naturally directs our attention to a few leading particulars relative to the Clifford family.[4] As before stated, they became possessed of their beautiful domain at the time of the Reformation. Although their descent was noble, yet when first located in our parish they simply ranked with the neighbouring gentry as to wealth and influence. The name of Anthony Clifford first occurs in the parish records in 1577. Thomas, his son, baptised at Chudleigh on 1st June, 1572 (afterwards Dr. Clifford), was a singular character; he had served in the army in the Netherlands, and had accompanied Robert, Earl of Essex, in his naval expedition to Cadiz. He applied himself to the study of theology at Oxford and took the degree of Doctor of Divinity. On the second of March, 1613, he was appointed afternoon lecturer in the Cathedral of Exeter, by the mayor and chamber, with a salary of fifty pounds per annum, and which was subsequently increased by the addition of ten pounds for the rent of his house. For three years he filled this office. On the twenty-sixth of November, 1625, Bishop Valentine Cary collated him to a prebend in the cathedral, and in the same year he was made a justice of the peace for the county of Devon. After this he preached without emolument *"to show others"* as he himself expressed it *"the way of avoiding those rocks whereon he in his youth had sometimes run"*. During his latter days he resided chiefly at Lower Bramble, which lies at the extremity of the parish of Ashton, between Chudleigh and Trusham. This estate was possessed by Dr. Clifford in right of his wife, one of the ancient family of Staplehill, in memory of whom there are some curious old monuments in Trusham church. He died 1634, aged sixty-two, and was buried in our chancel where there is a gravestone to his memory.

His son, Hugh Thomas, married Mary, eldest daughter of Sir George Chudleigh of Ashton, Bart. He was a colonel in the army of Charles I and served in his expedition against the Scots. His name frequently occurs in the records as he appears to have been deeply interested in the welfare of the parish, having undertaken the management of the erection of the alms houses, a source of anxiety to 'the seven men'. After his death the records give us the particulars of an interview on the 21st September, 1658 between his widow, who was also his executrix, and 'the seven men', which shows that Colonel Clifford's engagements with the parish were altogether unsettled at the time of his decease; the same record adds that though Thomas, his son, was *"no way liable as concerned his father's transactions"*, yet he was most anxious to unite with his mother in the final adjustment of the affair. This son, Thomas Clifford, was born at Ugbrooke, 1630. After a suitable education he was sent to Oxford, and was admitted a commoner of Exeter College. Leaving the university he entered the middle temple and afterwards travelled. In April, 1660 he was elected a burgess for Totnes and was knighted and re-elected the ensuing year. He distinguished himself by his gallantry in the Dutch war, and was conspicuous as diplomatist at the courts of Sweden and Denmark, as well as deeply involved in the intrigues carried on between Charles II and Louis XIV. His talents and eloquence were altogether of a superior order. We read in *Cliffordiana "that on the eighth of November, one thousand six hundred and sixty-six, his majesty delivered to him the white staff of comptroller of his household and, within a month later, named him a privy councillor. On the thirteenth of June, one thousand six hundred and sixty-eight, he gave him the appointment of treasurer to the household; and on the eighth of the following April declared him a Lord Commissioner of the Treasury. During Lord Arlington's absence in Holland, Sir Thomas Clifford was directed to execute the duties of his office as principal secretary of state. On the twenty-second of April, one thousand six hundred and seventy-two, the king raised him to the peerage, by the style and title of Baron of Chudleigh and, lastly, by special recommendation of His Royal Highness James, Duke of York, he was advanced to the most profitable office in the kingdom, viz. that of Lord Treasurer "*, so quickly did one preferment follow another. He was at the head of the government whose initials form the word 'cabal', a term somewhat expressive of their general policy and maladministration: their names were Clifford, Arlington, Buckingham, Ashley and Lauderdale.

Lord Clifford was finally made Lord High Treasurer of England, but did not long enjoy this new dignity; he died the following year, at the age of forty-three, and was interred in Ugbrooke chapel.

To him are his descendants indebted for their high position as peers of the realm, with a large amount of property; for we read in *Cliffordiana* that *"on the fifteenth of July, one thousand six hundred and seventy-two, the king granted him Cannington Priory, with its manor and rectory; also the manor of Fitzpain and the hundred of Cannington, with the free chapel of Piddlewaldeston. On the eighteenth of June, one thousand six hundred and seventy-three, he conveyed to him the perpetuity of the Craslow pastures, near Aylesbury, the lease of which for a term of sixty years he had granted him about two years before"*.

The records during the reign of James II present nothing of importance regarding the affairs of the parish. A unanimous invitation was sent in consequence of James' misrule to William, Prince of Orange, to occupy the throne of these realms. He landed at Brixham on the 5th November, 1688 and slept in Chudleigh on the second night at the mansion of the Cholwichs in the centre of the town. He, from one of the windows, harangued the inhabitants in broken English, if not to their edification, at least to their satisfaction, for he was universally hailed as the deliverer of the country from religious persecution, anarchy and oppression.

About this period the family of Woolcombe were resident in Chudleigh and their name is of frequent occurrence in the parish register. Robert Woolcombe, M.A., was a remarkable character and a few particulars concerning him cannot but prove interesting. He was presented to the living of Moreton by one of the Courtenay family and ordained at Dartmouth in 1657: 'he was a hard student, a great philosopher, a sound solid preacher, and a courageous advocate of non-conformity; for this he lost not only a good benefice, but a good estate, being ejected from his living in one thousand six hundred and sixty-two, and his father disinherited him, making his son his heir, and charging in his will that he should not have the educating of him'. Mr. Woolcombe on his ejectment, was followed by a few of his hearers, and became the founder of the Presbyterian Church at Moreton. He had, with his congregation, to endure severe persecution; he was, by the Five-Mile-Act, expelled from the town and on his return to visit his little flock was seized and committed to prison. This persecution lasted till 1687 when Mr. Woolcombe and eleven others procured a license, dated at Whitehall signed Sunderland; for this a considerable sum was extorted. This license became useless almost immediately after by the passing of the Toleration Act: 'amidst all these conflicts and persecutions, Mr. Woolcombe found a good conscience a continual feast, living contentedly and dying at peace in his house at Chudleigh in one thousand six hundred and ninety-two'.

The records from this period being simply parish accounts, no longer furnish matters of local interest. 'The seven men' continued to be elected even towards the close of the eighteenth century and a majority of their names were to be seen attached to notices relating to parish affairs in conjunction with the overseers and churchwardens. The woollen trade, so long a source of profitable industry to the inhabitants of Chudleigh and the neighbourhood, gradually declined.

The loss of a flourishing manufacture for which nothing could compensate was soon felt in the waning prosperity of the middle and working classes, and a continued diminution of the tolls of the fairs and markets which have finally become but of little value.

Westcote describes Chudleigh as *"an ancient market town frequented with great resort of neighbour parishes every Saturday"*. The fairs were also considerable; they were held on Easter Tuesday, and the third Thursday and Friday in June, which was a large sheep and lamb fair; and the second day was noted for the sale of scythes, reaping hooks and implements of husbandry. The third fair was on the 2nd October. The Easter is the only one of the three that retains its importance, and there is still a considerable show of cattle in the play-park. The market, so important, is now sunk into comparative insignificance and the town, having lost its trade, is no longer a 'resort for neighbour parishes'.

1. Bombast, a kind of fustian.
2. Armour.
3. Nicholas Vaughan, gentleman, elected about this time as a muster master to the city of Exeter, at a pension of £6 per annum.
4. See description of paintings, pages 84-89.

CHAPTER IV

The Bishop's Palace was situated south of the town, within a few paces of the romantic rock, on an eminence united to its summit, which extended across the vale. It was surrounded by rich pastures stretching from the church to the parish boundary of the Teign. On the east lay the dell with its woody copse and immediately beyond, Ugbrooke Park; the last formed a portion of the ecclesiastical property, and the Precentor was permitted to reside in it for the convenience of collecting the manorial dues. The palace was reached by a gradual ascent and, although thus elevated, was sheltered on all sides but the south-west. Most of our baronial and princely structures, even when crumbling into dust, have still left some walls to define their extent or some distinct features to show by their style of architecture the different stages of their advancement. Here, on the contrary, the merciless hand of time and the avarice of man have left but a few fragments of what for centuries adorned the neighbourhood, and must have been a grand and imposing structure.

The palace and the chapel dedicated to St. Michael extended nearly the whole width of what is now an orchard. All that remains of the palace are some stone steps, and portions of three apartments arched over, with their original heavy stone work. These are now thatched and converted into cellars for the use of the farm. Tradition says that beneath the ruins there are some dismal vaults or dungeons; if such there be, they were alike common to all palaces and castles built at the same period, and were the necessary strongholds for thieves and malefactors, as the punishment of evil doers was vested in the lords of manors. In a line with the palace, and separated from it by an open area, lay the chapel; these buildings appeared to have been connected on the west by a high wall that enclosed the area. The palace evidently faced the hanging woods of the romantic and beautiful dell. A coin of the wall of some height and immense thickness is all that now remains of the chapel. The most perfect of the ruins are the boundary walls that, towards the south-west, has in it arched loop holes of highly finished masonry. These command an extensive view of the country south and are placed at regular distances, similar to those met with on fortified walls, often with the addition of towers. Adjoining this boundary was probably situated the portcullis gate, by which the palace area was entered. The accumulation of soil in which these ruins are concealed is immense; it hides more than half the western wall and most probably belonged to a stately 'plaisaunce' with parterres and terraces extending without doubt to the summit of the rock, such as were generally found surrounding all the palaces and religious houses of the Catholics. Men shutting themselves up from the business of the world took refuge in their gardens, and on them bestowed much time and energy. It is probable from the early mention of the palace in the records of the Cathedral Church of Exeter, that it was erected about the year 1100. This and the following century (as is well-known) are styled the age of architecture; a vast number of religious edifices were then built throughout the kingdom and, in consequence, a great improvement was observable in their style.

The burying ground, one of the important appendages to the chapel, lay in the eastern corner of the orchard, as here some skeletons were dug up when the road to the quarry was recently widened. The ancient flour mill was connected with the 'plaisaunce' by a narrow pathway and wall, a part of which was also standing until of late. The flour mill was the necessary accompaniment to ecclesiastical establishments, as the early bishops and abbots had frequently to supply the wants of the poor as well as to provide for their own numerous retinue. A well and spring in the vicinity of the palace still retain the names of Bishop's Well and St. Mary's Spring.

The principal entrance to this domain from the western road was through a noble gothic arched gateway, about the site of the garden now belonging to the palace cottage. This gateway was taken down within the memory of some of the present inhabitants; its demolition must be a source of some regret to all who were admirers of interesting relics of bygone days. The space between this entrance and the palace was considerable and was probably adorned with groves and alleys. The present site of the modern cottage may have been that of the offices and stables. An antiquarian aided in his investigation of these ruins on removing the soil by which they are covered, might unravel much that concerned their original grandeur and extent, and portray them more minutely. No description of what the palace and chapel were in their palmy days is extant. The few records of historians only refer to their utter ruin and desolation. Risdon thus writes: *"the bishops of this diocese had a sumptuous seat here, with the manor thereunto belonging, part of which structure yet standeth, which only numbereth what large possessions once they had, and how little they now enjoy in this place"*. Lysons writes: *"at Chudleigh are several walls and arches which belonged to the bishops of Exeter at that place"*; such are the sole remains of this once magnificent abode of priestly grandeur. Its massive arches, marble pillars and the materials which composed the walls were sold and used for different purposes; some were thrown into the adjoining kiln and converted into lime.

According to Dr. Oliver, this palace was a favourite residence of the early bishops. It must have strikingly contrasted in beauty of situation and elegance of structure with their dull abode at Exeter, but how is the scene changed? The lovely 'plaisaunce', with its parterres and terraces, are no longer decked with choice flowers. The apartments in which an anxious audience once listened to the precepts, hung on the consolations, or awaited the commands of their priestly lords, are now desolate; its literal and pretended foundation on a rock has not prevented its fall. Within the walls of the chapel dedicated to St. Michael, there must have been enjoyed many seasons of rapt devotion in the celebration of high mass, and the awe inspiring ceremonies of the Church of Rome. Many expensive obits and solemn requiems have been there chanted for the souls of the departed. Many ordinations have there added the sons of the wealthy and noble to the Catholic priesthood. Imagination may lend an ear to the chanted matin, rising with morning's dawn, and the *'Ave-Maria'* mingling with the shades of evening. In the silent hour of midnight the rock itself has witness without doubt the infliction of many a severe penance, and the sustentation of many a lengthened vigil. With the death of Bishop Lacy in 1455, and the departure of his remains from the palace, it appeared as though 'Ichabod' were inscribed on its walls; no further mention is made of it until sold by Bishop Veysey at the Reformation.

From the occasional residence of the bishops of Exeter at the palace, the town was indebted for a supply of running water obtained from a distance; a few particulars concerning the interesting fact will next claim attention. Chudleigh, by its natural position, was deprived of this important essential to cleanliness and comfort. It is true that it had brooks, but they flowed in the vallies, and were only available by steep ascents and descents. We have no record as to the period in which this great boon was obtained, or any particulars concerning its accomplishment. Tradition ascribes it to Bishop Lacy who, according to Izacke, *"well governed the church thirty-five years from one thousand four hundred and twenty"*. It has always been considered to have been effected for the accommodation of the palace, at the same time giving the inhabitants a participation in its advantages. The source of the spring was found under Haldon in a dingle now belonging to M.E.N. Parker, Esquire. Before diverted by a weir, it flowed towards Bramble Brook which falls into the Teign at Crocombe bridge. The new channel marked out for this little stream was ably and judiciously executed. It flows nearly parallel with the new Exeter road as far as Heathfield Cottage; but here it was on an eminence east of Chudleigh, and had therefore after being carried across the old road, to pursue a winding and retrograde course, until brought to a right level, for again being turned towards Chudleigh. It was then made to flow on to a pleasant path-field situated at the top of Exeter Street; here it may be considered as waiting disposal for the good of the town. For nearly two centuries it poured a part of its treasures (on its way to the palace) into a large stone trough at the bottom of Culver Street. In 1601, from an entry in the parochial register, we find that 'the seven men' made a new 'shoute' for the accommodation of the west end of the town, the expenses of which are thus summed up: *"workmens wages and theer dyett as appeareth from theer books in pticular four pounds thirteen shillings and fourpence"*. To supply this 'shoute' a part of the stream was diverted from meadows still called Shute-lands, as wending its way to the Bishop's palace, where it evidently formed a fish pond, which was often found in connection with the early Catholic establishments. Another entry shows that the Pot-water, as it is called, claimed the particular attention of 'the seven men'; item, *"pd. for redding of the towne leate from the hedd wear unto the newe shoute at the west end of the towne, twice this two years, fourteen shillings and eightpence"*. This stream is now under the control of a committee appointed by the parish, yearly, on the 22nd day of May. Instead of pouring its treasures into a stone trough, they now flow through a conduit connected with the granite pillar in the centre of the town, and are otherwise so guided and distributed as to afford a supply to all the inhabitants. The source under Haldon is about three miles distance, which is considerably increased by its winding course, as it is carried through more than twenty fields and crosses in its way five different roads. The work, considering the early period of its accomplishment, was one of considerable skill and labour. While the palace itself has decayed, and the name even of the benefactor who originated and completed this important work is in obscurity, the stream drawing on nature's exhaustless treasury has for nearly five centuries pursued its quiet way, refreshing man and beast with one of the essentials of natural life.

The Woollen Trade, once extensively carried on and intimately connected for centuries with our ancient town, requires a few remarks and naturally induces a few observations as to the cause of its final abandonment. The rapid progress made in modern discoveries, of which machinery is the crowning point, and the application of this most important branch of mechanism, has its particular bearing on the subject. The ability of applying and equally distributing force by human hands without the operation of machinery is very limited, and in all our works of art it is found necessary in the present age to call in the aid of mechanical power of one kind or another. Those who have taken the lead in reducing to practice the modern improvements in manufacturing science have not only been themselves rewarded by the accumulation of wealth, but have conferred on their immediate localities a great amount of good by their encouragement of an enlightened and concentrated industry. As an instance of this, the application of spindles and shuttles driven without hands have secured for the enterprising inhabitants of Yorkshire the transfer of a trade that once had its principal seats amid the rural scenes of Devon. It is true that a particular branch of the trade still exists at Buckfastleigh, Ashburton and a few other towns, but even at these places, where experienced hands and considerable capital are employed, the trade flags, and every year sees rather a diminution than an increase.

There can be no hesitation in ascribing to Chudleigh an early and important share of this trade. All the middle and labouring classes, as well as many of the wealthy farmers belonging to neighbouring parishes, were in one way or another connected with it. No public or private local record exists respecting the particular sort of flannel or serge manufactured, but it was well known to merchants formerly carrying on the trade in Devon that its ancient fabrics were of a peculiar and excellent kind, and bore the name of 'Chudleighs', not only at the time, but long after they had ceased to be made at that place where they had originated and been brought to perfection. There are still a few of the aged inhabitants who recollect when processions of woolcombers clothed in woollen caps and gowns paraded the town on particular days, the elder of the fraternity being equipped as Bishop Blaize (the patron saint of the trade), with a mitre on his head; so completely is the scene changed that the past appears rather as a dream than reality. The slight information that oral tradition supplies refers altogether to the days of its decline and final abandonment. Mr Moore, in his history of Devon, has ably traced out the origin, rise and decline of the woollen trade; a few short extracts will throw much light on the subject and cannot but prove highly interesting.

"The manufacture of woollen cloth in Devon, as well as England in general, appears to have been derived from Flanders and the Low Countries. No mention is made of fulling mills in this county in the Doomsday survey; but from their being noticed in the records of Edward the First, who granted charters to foreign merchants and manufacturers, for the purpose of settling in the kingdom, it is evident that cloth was made in Exeter and Chudleigh." Here we see Chudleigh is mentioned in connection with Exeter as manufacturing cloths at this early period. *"Edward the Third also by the measures he adopted*

for the encouragement of manufactories, contributed greatly towards laying the foundation of our national superiority; he gave great encouragement to weavers of woollen cloths, as well as dyers and fullers from the continent, who came to London, and afterwards settled in different parts of the kingdom. It is known that a wool-staple existed in Exeter, in one thousand three hundred and fifty-four; from this period the trade gradually increased in importance throughout the county, and many eminent clothiers were not long after to be found in the principal towns." Exeter rose to be the greatest wool market in England: *"its ordinary sales of wool on Fridays amounted to the value of ten thousand pounds sterling"*. Westcote clearly describes the state of the trade in his days and, after tracing its progress and the description of goods then manufactured, adds: *"first the gentleman farmer, or husbandman, sends his wool to the market, which is bought either by the comber or spinster, and they, the next week, bring it thither again in yarn, which the weaver buys; and on the market following brings it thither again in cloth, where it is sold either to the clothier (who sends it to London) or to the merchant who (after it hath passed the fuller's mill, and sometimes the dyer's vat) transports it. The large quantities whereof cannot be well guessed at, but best known to the custom-book whereunto it yields no small commodity, and this is continued all the year throughout"*.

The great increase of the woollen manufacture in the seventeenth century (Mr. Moore again observes) *"was occasioned by the revival or extension of the sale of English cloth in Italy, Turkey and the Levant"*. Morrison, who was in Turkey in 1596, speaks of *"Kerseys and Tin as our chief articles of commerce in that market. The East India trade was at one time immense; from one thousand seven hundred and ninety-five to one thousand eight hundred and five the average of their purchases was two hundred and fifty to three hundred thousand pieces annually"*, each piece containing twenty-six yards, called long ells. In this branch and the Turkey trade Chudleigh was chiefly concerned.

In addition to this brief sketch of the once flourishing state of the woollen trade generally throughout the county, it may be added as a reference to Chudleigh itself that Mr. John Pulling, who died about a century ago, was the last of our original woolstaplers and clothiers. The wool combers, spinners, weavers and all he employed or with whom acquainted, ever cherished the most lively recollections of his equity and benevolence. His sons continued to carry on the trade (though greatly curtailed) and finally relinquished it altogether.

Messrs Bailey and Leare, at a later period, converted Oil-park flour mills into a woollen factory and spun worsted for the weavers. They were succeeded by a Mr. Bampford who belonged to a highly respectable firm in Somersetshire: although carried on by him somewhat extensively, proved far from lucrative, and at his decease was relinquished. Mr. Pearce of Exeter next rented these mills for about ten years, when the trade was finally abandoned in 1830.

Not a loom is now to be met with in the town where they could be once seen through the old-fashioned lattice windows of almost every poor dwelling, while their attendant, the spinning-wheel, went round and round at the respective cottage doors. The woollen trade is lost to this county with no hope of revival, the teeming population of the north, with an abundance of fuel at command, and all the united advantages of combined industry, having left our towns far behind in ingenuity, wealth and intellectual attainments.

Before entering on the subject of the Chudleigh fire, it appears necessary to observe that there belonged to the old town mansions of considerable antiquity. The residence of the Cholwichs formed a large court in the middle of the town. Near the church there was another large house with handsome oriel windows; these, with other buildings, were illustrated in a series of published views by Le Cort, a French artist. The market-house was a long straggling building in the centre of the town and was taken down and rebuilt not long before the fire; attached to it there was a fine old town-cross, a flight of steps forming its base. The workhouse opposite the church was one of the most ancient buildings in the town. From its dilapidated condition, and the miserable accommodation it afforded its poor denizens, it was taken down and rebuilt at a considerable expense to the parish in 1818. The alms houses at the entrance of Pottery Lane built by 'the seven men', consisted of two storeys of five rooms each with a wooden gallery outside leading to the upper apartments, were sold by the parish and taken down in 1820.

On the 22nd May, 1807, after a long continuance of fine weather when all was sunny and tranquil, and the inhabitants of Chudleigh were busily engaged in their usual avocations, at twelve o'clock the cry of fire arose. It broke out at a bakehouse in Culver Street; the flames immediately spread to Mill Lane, then across to Exeter Street in which stood the King's Arms Inn, one of the important posting-houses of the town, much in request from the travelling consequent on the war. The stables and back premises of this inn, as throughout the town, were thatched, and in many instances were on fire before the dwelling-houses. The affrighted inhabitants thus found themselves hemmed in with flames, while endeavouring to save their goods, and had only just time to escape, leaving much valued treasure behind. A strong breeze springing up from the east, the flames extended with fearful rapidity; three streets were at once on fire, while large flakes of burning materials were carried to all parts of the town. The market-house, rebuilt and slated not long before, appeared to the inhabitants a safe depot for their goods, and it was accordingly soon filled; not however to the safety of what was there deposited, but to the destruction of both, as portions of goods were carried in on fire and the whole was quickly in a blaze. The fire engine had been taken out but, either from excess of heat or want of water, was immediately abandoned as useless. To the terror-stricken inhabitants the place seemed doomed to utter destruction, and they must have felt that no effort of theirs could in any way avail in rescuing it. At two o'clock a barrel of gunpowder (kept for fusing the lime rocks) exploded, and shook the town to its centre, at the same time giving a fresh impetus to the flames, while it added to the general consternation and scattered portions of books and papers more than a mile distant.

As the fire in the centre of the town abated, where the flames had raged in terrific grandeur, it was deemed advisable to pull down a few houses to intercept the fire in order to save if possible the extremities of the town. Persons were by this time assembled from the neighbourhood and with their assistance this was promptly done, but not before nearly two-thirds of the town was consumed. The fire that thus very nearly swept the town from one end to the other, and scarcely left a vestige of its most ancient habitations, occupied a period of about only four hours.

Time would fail to relate all the circumstances connected with this tragic drama. Of all the hairbreadth escapes of those who (with what they considered valuable) rushed hither and thither through the flames, many even having their clothes burnt on their backs, of sleeping infants in cradles and the aged almost as helpless, who were removed from one supposed place of safety to another, of anxious housewives who were loaded with china and glass, which they threw hastily down and smashed, while much that was really valuable and substantial was left a prey to the devouring element. The mortal remains of an old and respected inhabitant who had died suddenly at some little distance, had the previous day been brought back to his own habitation near the centre of the town. On the cry of fire the coffin was removed into the street when the son of the deceased, with an affectionate solicitude stronger even than death itself, rushed through the flames from his own habitation which was on fire and tore off the burning pall that covered the coffin; then with the aid of a few friends hurried it to the churchyard, where the remains were hastily interred by the vicar, two mourners, being all that could be spared from the appalling conflagration, to attend the dead to its final resting place. It was truly a fortunate circumstance that not a human life was lost amidst all the confusion of this awful scene: night and darkness would have added tenfold to its horrors. The coaches accustomed to pass through about mid-day were compelled to take a circuitous route to Haldon, through the play-park, adjoining meadow and up the Teignmouth Hill by way of Bridgelands. One valuable horse and a pig which could not be extricated perished.

The church was made a temporary resting place for the houseless inhabitants, where they mourned over the loss of their long hoarded treasures, and lamented their forlorn and destitute condition. Tents were afterwards erected in adjoining fields for those who were utterly destitute, while the more fortunate were accommodated in the dwellings of their relatives and friends.

It is pleasing to turn from all this misery to the unbounded benevolence manifested on this melancholy occasion. The sympathy of the gentry of surrounding parishes was greatly excited and clothes and food were poured into the town in abundance. The masonic fraternity of Teignmouth sent cart-loads of bread and beer for the necessitous. The bell of the town-cryer almost daily announced the arrival of these welcome and generous supplies which were distributed in the play-park. There were boxes fixed at each end of the town to receive the contributions of the many hundreds who came on the following sabbath from all parts. Subscription lists were opened far and near, and the liberality of the public was unbounded. £21,000 were subscribed, besides much private charity in money, clothes, bibles and prayer books, which had no public record. The leading men of the parish formed themselves into a committee, with Lord Clifford as chairman, to consider the most effectual means of affording relief to the sufferers. The committee had no easy task in the distribution of such an immense sum, and their difficulties were greatly increased by strife and disunion among themselves. There was also much trouble in checking the avarice of many who swelled their losses to an amount altogether beyond the bounds of probability. One of the most able and indefatigable of the committee thus addresses Lord Clifford in the preface attached to the financial report of the various sums awarded: *"in adjusting claims so multifarious and complicated, it cannot but be supposed but that some impositions may have been practised with success"*. On an inspection of the list we must feel surprised at the immense sums awarded to a few particular individuals, as also at the names of many wealthy persons as participators in public charity. It cannot but be regretted that a committee who had so much power and money at command, had not exercised it in securing for the town buildings of architectural strength and uniformity, and thus have made Chudleigh as beautiful in itself, as it is remarkable for its salubrious and delightful situation. It is also a matter of regret that no memorial as a tablet or public building was erected in remembrance of an event which gave the inhabitants a considerable amount of wealth, and enabled them without delay to rebuild the town, affording them in exchange new and convenient habitations for what were altogether the reverse.

The Chudleigh fire which we have thus endeavoured faintly to portray (for it indeed baffles description) was for years an endless theme of conversation, and to some extent is even now a date for past events, *"before and after the fire"* may literally be termed household words. If ever a town owed a deep debt of gratitude for responsive sympathy promptly manifested in unbounded acts of liberality it is Chudleigh, and though there is no record of its gratitude to be found inscribed on marble or brass, the recollection can never be effaced from its private annals.

As travelling is in some degree familiar to us all, it may not be uninteresting here to make a few brief remarks on the former state of the roads in this neighbourhood. In no branch of art do our ancestors appear more deficient than in that of making roads and keeping them in repair. If a hill presented itself, the possibility of turning the road otherwise than across the highest part was never thought of; also equally deficient, in making roads pursue the most direct course to the desired point; indeed, they seemed to think (if we may judge from their lanes) that the longest way round was the shortest way home; they were also equally indifferent as to the ruts and stones, the great impediments to safe travelling. This state of things continued with some little modification to 1815 when a Scotchman named Mac Adam turned his whole attention to the subject, and the result is the hard convex roads which we now enjoy, termed 'Macadamised'. Many of the present generation may remember the conveyance of all kinds of heavy goods by pack horses: a number of these might be seen in a line, jogging along these narrow and winding paths, the head horse bearing a bell, by the tinkling sound of which the cavalcade was kept together and prevented from straggling at nightfall. This rude and inconvenient method of carriage continued till the latter part of the last century when one-horse carts came into general use.

The great western road had its course through Chudleigh from a comparatively early period; it is noticed by Westcote as a *"great thoroughfare lying in the high-way from Plymouth to Exeter"*. This route from Chudleigh was formerly up the hill called Heathfield Lakes. It cannot but excite our wonder that such dangerous hilly roads were in use even to a recent date. The long slow coaches drawn by four and sometimes six horses had during the war to toil up this and similar hills on their way to and from Plymouth, to the no small risk and terror of the travellers. From Exeter to Plymouth the journey occupied a long day, or rather fourteen hours, a distance of only forty-six miles.

The Pottery Lane or old way, was the original path to Chudleigh Bridge. Chudleigh had no communication with Newton, or the South Hams in former days, except by crossing Heightly Bridge, situated east of Chudleigh Bridge up Sheppards Hill, which as of yore is almost perpendicular. The present road to Newton following the course of the Teign, is nearly level; it gave a new route to Plymouth.

From parish to parish the paths were all but impassable; that to Ashton after crossing Crocombe Bridge, was contiguous to the river. It was often overflown and almost as rough as the bed of the Teign itself. The roads to the neighbouring parishes that were alike impassable for vehicles, are now excellent.

The romantic old bridge over the Teign was taken down in 1816. It is thus described by Polwhele: *"Chiddely Bridge as Leland calls it, is a county bridge. It consists of two large arches and one very small, to draw off the water"*. Whatever these historians thought of it, this county bridge was narrow, the walls low, the approach at each end was by a sharp turn; its passage was altogether dangerous for the long heavy laden coaches. It had angular recesses for the protection of foot passengers if overtaken while crossing it. Its foundation stones are still visible a little above the site of the present elegant granite bridge which, with one spacious arch of considerable elevation, spans the river in a direct line with the descent from Chudleigh. The inconvenience arising from the rough and hilly state of the road to Exeter was not remedied until 1822 when a new road was cut over Haldon towards Kennford. The travelling through Chudleigh after its completion was very great; it included six royal mails, a number of stagecoaches and a variety of other vehicles.

Among the vicissitudes that have befallen our little town, the last and not the least, is the loss of wealth and activity, incident on its former importance as belonging to the great western thoroughfare, the opening of the South Devon railroad superseding it almost entirely and leaving the town in rural seclusion.

CHAPTER V

In the Southern Division of Devon, in the Hundred of Exminster, and the Deanery of Kenn, on the great western road to Plymouth and 182 miles from London, is situated the well-known town of Chudleigh. The parish extends about four miles from north to south, and about three and a half from east to west, containing 6230 acres. The population according to the last census was 2401, and the town comprises about five hundred houses. It is built on an eminence belonging to the western side of a vale that stretches towards the Teign and Knighton Heath. It may be well said that this little town is beautiful for situation, 'set on a hill' in the midst of a continuous descent, a peculiarity that gives to it an air of cheerfulness and importance, and makes it a pleasing object from whatever direction it is beheld. Had commissioners in connection with the present sanitary movement been invited to select a spot on which to build, none could have been found more healthy or cheerful than this chosen by our rude ancestors.

The surrounding parishes lie as follows: Kenn and a part of Exminster, north and north-east; Trusham and Ashton, north and north-west, from which parishes it is separated by Bramble-brook which falls into the Teign at Crocombe Bridge; Hennock, west and south-west, divided by the Teign; Kingsteignton, south; Ideford, further east, and Ashcombe, north-east, where it finally joins Kenton. These different parishes encircle Chudleigh, although some of them are distanced by Haldon whose barren acres are divided between them and Chudleigh.

Its western boundary, the Teign (anciently written and now generally pronounced *Ting,*[1] so called by the Britons, for that 'it is narrowly pent with narrow banks') is thus described by Lysons: *"rises*

*on the borders of Dartmoor with two heads meeting near Holy-street,
Chagford, near Whiddon Park and Moreton Woods, near Dunsford,
Christow, Hennock, Chudleigh-Knighton and Teigngrace, where on
an estate called Teignyeo it is joined by the Bovey-river, thence to
Kingsteignton; hereabouts it becomes a wide estuary and falls into
the sea between Shaldon and Teignmouth, its course having been
about thirty miles".*

Polwhele, when exploring this parish, appears to have been
altogether overcome with the beauty of the scenery around Chudleigh
and rather singularly writes as follows: *"For the picturesque views
which this parish affords, they are really so romantic as to beggar
description"*; however, some idea may be conveyed of what really
constitutes its picturesque beauty when a brief outline of some of its
principal features is given. On the east the vale is bounded by rising
ground of uniform elevation through which may be traced an irregular
stratum of mountain lime rock reaching to the foot of Haldon. This
high tract of land is crowned with the richly wooded confines of
Ugbrooke Park; after sheltering the town, it is expanded and
interspersed with the lime rocks that rise to a considerable elevation;
surrounded by trees, their tops clothed with mountain plants and lively
verdure, while immediately beyond rises Haldon, its barren line
forming a striking contrast to the rich vale below. On the west the
view consists of alternate hill and dale; extending far beyond the
boundary of the parish, it includes the vale of the Teign, interspersed
with rich pastures, a succession of hills terminating in the distant tors
of Dartmoor. Towards the south-east another scene of indescribable
beauty presents itself as luxuriant as Haytor is wild. The scenery
around Chudleigh can vie with any of the most admired spots of
Devon, or even England. The wonders of the Peak and the lakes of
Westmoreland may have some superlative points of attraction, and

all the charms that the genius of poetry can throw around them, but here nothing is wanting to excite the mind of the enraptured admirer of rural scenery.

Humboldt includes the south of England with several delightful regions of the earth such as Brittany, Normandy, Guernsey and Jersey as distinguished by the mildness of their winters, and the low temperature and clouded skies of their summers, forming a striking contrast to the climate of the interior of Eastern Europe. These beautiful spring and summer clouds (*"as they are variously moulded by the sun"*) fling their deep shadows on the hills around, momentarily altering the features of the landscape; then, as they glide from hill to hill, delight while they astonish the beholder by their transforming effect, and prove how justly it has been observed, *"that the clouds themselves are often characteristic and animating features of the prospect"*.

The air in this neighbourhood is considered peculiarly dry and bracing as well as genial, the eastern series of limestone hills contributing greatly to its salubrity. Fogs are seldom felt within its precincts, and the town is raised above the humid vapour of the Teign. The south and south-west winds prevail here as in the south of Devon, generally a considerable portion of the year; to them our town is completely exposed but, although they are rude and boisterous, they are seldom cold or piercing. On the contrary, the westerly breezes that reach this vale from Dartmoor softened by the woody tract over which they pass become pure, fresh and elastic, and thus invigorate the many invalids who are recommended here, as a change from the relaxing heats of the southern coast. They have often literally proved gales of health to numbers perfectly restored after a month's residence in this neighbourhood.

In common with other parts of Devon, spring commences and

fruits ripen earlier than elsewhere in England, with the exception of a few favoured localities such as Penzance. The beautiful private gardens of the town have many delicate shrubs surviving the winter without extra care. The writer is not aware that any registers exist determining the quantity of rain that falls, or the actual state of the temperature throughout the year.

After crossing Haldon, Chudleigh is approached on the north by a beautiful and gradual descent of three miles; the town is then entered by a steep ascent. The first object that meets the eye is a noble row of elm trees of equal growth surrounding the church. The town at its first survey appears to consist of one main street of considerable length but, in fact, there are three that run parallel to the centre. These are Culver Street by which the town is now entered from the north, Exeter Street once the principal thoroughfare, and Wood Way, chiefly tenanted by the poorer inhabitants. In the centre of the town there is a triangular space where the old market-house formerly stood; now there is a granite pillar of recent erection to which are attached a pump and conduit. From this area a street branches off to the south-east known by the appellation, Mill Lane, and leading to the beautiful watering places of Teignmouth and Dawlish, about seven miles distant. The remaining part of the town consists of a wide and pleasant street. The pavements that were rough and uneven are now being gradually flagged with hewn stone from the marble quarries. The houses are chiefly built of stone, its native material, and the town presents a neat and cheerful appearance. No building speculation has been carried on to any extent, as in many towns less favoured. The commodious habitations belonging to Chudleigh have been chiefly built by their wealthy proprietors.

The church is a venerable gothic pile, built of limestone interspersed with red sandstone, and in some parts coped with granite.

The south aisle is crowned with granite battlements and a bold moulding underneath of the same material, and the mullions of the windows on that side of the church are granite also. The windows in the chancel are formed of red stone and all the others of freestone. The tower is a substantial edifice evidently intended, from its shape and solidity, to have been surmounted with a spire, but the summit is finished with a dwarf pointed roof, covered with slate, which contains six harmonious bells.

The whole of the external walls of the church and tower were, until lately, covered with roughcast, which disfigured their beauty and concealed their architecture. Now, however, this unsightly coating has been removed, the walls neatly pointed, and the venerable fabric is presented to the spectator in its original purity. The church is dedicated to St. Martin and St. Mary and is very ancient. No exact account of the date of its erection exists. Dr. Oliver, in his Ecclesiastical Antiquities, states that the first mention of Chudleigh Church as belonging to the See of Exeter *"is in a deed of Bishop Bartholomew (between the years one thousand one hundred and sixty-one and one thousand one hundred and eighty-four). This church also forms the subject of a deed of John, Bishop of Exeter (between the years one thousand one hundred and eighty-six and one thousand one hundred and ninety-one). The parish church under the patronage of St. Martin and St. Mary, though at various times since partially altered, was dedicated by Bishop Bronscombe on the sixth of November, one thousand two hundred and fifty-nine"*. It consists of a nave, chancel,[2] a south aisle supported by eight granite pillars, and a north transept commonly called Hunt's Aisle. It measures in length 110 feet and 56 at its greatest breadth. Many of the old pews were for a considerable number of years in a dilapidated state, and formed a most unsightly assemblage of irregular unseemly boxes of various heights, inclinations and dimensions; containing with the galleries accommodation for 648 persons, and the condition of the interior was anything but creditable to the parishioners.

In 1843, however, they were fully awakened to the necessity of rendering the House of God more convenient and more in accordance with its high and holy purposes, and proceeded to the goodly work with energy and zeal. £800 was borrowed of the public works commissioners, on a mortgage of the rates, to which the dissenters of all denominations liberally consented, and the subscription lists soon swelled to a considerable amount, and the total outlay on the works has reached near £1700, and the church in lieu of being a reproach to the parish, is now one of the most beautiful in the diocese. It has been newly pewed throughout, the galleries have been rebuilt, the fine old screen restored, and the chancel and its fittings entirely remodelled. The principal entrance to the church was originally on the north side; this has been blocked up and by the uniform arrangement of the pews, the sittings have been increased to 753, of which 250 are free and unappropriated.

The chief entrance to the church is now by a handsome gothic archway in the tower. The first object that strikes the spectator on entering the building is the splendid east window of stained glass. This beautiful ornament of the church was placed there at the sole cost of John Williams, Esquire as a memorial to his esteemed friend, the late Rev. Gilbert Burrington, for fifty five years the vicar of the parish. It is of the decorated style of English architecture and consists of five lights. The centre represents our Saviour crowned, beneath which is the crucifixion; on the right are the figures of St. Peter and St. Paul, above whom in medallions are representations of the Nativity and our Lord's Baptism, and under them The Agony in the Garden and Christ bearing his Cross; on the left side are figures of St. James and St. John; above are medallions uniform with the right side, descriptive of our Saviour washing his disciples' feet, and the Last Supper, and beneath them the Resurrection and the Ascension. In the upper corner on the right is a figure of St. Martin, dividing his cloak with a beggar; and on the left the figure of the Virgin Mary, who are as before stated the patron saints of the church. The head of the window is filled with devices emblematic of the Trinity and Crucifixion, and at the base is the following inscription: *"In honorem Dei et in piam memoriam Gilberti Burrington LV. annos hujus parochiae Vicarii dedicat Johannes Williams, anno sacro MDCCCXLVII"*.

The east end of the southern aisle[3]. has lately been adorned by an elegant stained window representing the Transfiguration. It contains three lights: the centre having the figure of our Saviour, the right that of Moses, the left that of Elias; and on the base the figures of Peter, James and John are vividly portrayed. This beautiful addition to the church was made by Admiral Sir David Dunn in memory of the late Lady Dunn, whose estimable qualities were appreciated by all who knew her. The following is the inscription: *"In pious memory of Louisa Henrietta Dunn, died A.D. MDCCCXLIX"*.

The principal contributors to the restoration of the church were Mrs. Parker, Mr. Parker, Mr. Williams, Mr. Yarde, the Rev. W.H. Palk (the vicar), and the Rev. Chas. M. Edward Collins. The monuments in the church deserving notice are but few. That erected to the memory of James Eastchurch in the south aisle and that to Sir Pierce Courtenay and his lady in the chancel are the most striking and are more fully described hereafter. The former has been recently restored to its original condition, but the latter still needs the hand of the skilful artificer. In the north aisle there is an old portrait belonging to one of the Hunt family; it bears date 1601; it has been lately restored at the expense of

Mr. Parker. This aisle was probably appropriated to the Hunts from their first residence in the parish, and still retains their name.

In removing some of the old pews from the screen, some curious paintings were discovered, twenty in number, representing the apostles and prophets, each having a Latin inscription (the English translation is added for the general reader) in the following order:-

1. *Petrus.* Credo in Deum Patrem omnipotentem Creatorem coeli et terrae.
Peter. I believe in God the Father Almighty, Creator of heaven and earth.

2. *Jeremias.* Patrem invocabitis qui fecit coelum et terram.
Jeremiah. Ye shall call me my Father who made heaven and earth.

3. *Andreas.* Et in Jesum Christum Filium ejus unicum Dominum nostrum.
Andrew. And in Jesus Christ, his only Son our Lord.

4. *Paulus.* Deus dixit ad me filius meus es tu ego hodie genui te.
Paul. God has said unto me thou art my Son this day have I begotten thee.

5. *Jacobus Major.* Qui conceptus est de Spiritu Sancto natus ex Maria Virgine.
James the elder. Who was conceived by the Holy Ghost, born of the Virgin Mary.

6. *Ysaias.* Ecce Virgo concipiet et pariet filium.
Isaiah. Behold a Virgin shall conceive and bear a Son.

7. *Johnes Evangl.* Passus sub Pontio Pilato crucifixus mortuus et sepultus.
John the Evangelist. He suffered under Pontius Pilate, was crucified dead and buried.

8. *Zacharias.* Aspicient illi eum qui crucifixerunt.
Zachariah. They shall look on Him whom they have crucified.

9. *Thomas. Descendit ad inferos tertia die resurget.*
Thomas. He descended into hell, and the third day he shall rise again.

10.*Oseas.* O mors ero mors tua morsus tuus ero inferus.
Hosea. O death I will be thy plague, O grave I will be thy destruction.

11.*Jacobus.* Ascendit ad coelos sedet ad dexteram Patris.
Jacob. He hath ascended into heaven and sitteth at the right hand of God.

12.*Amos.* Qui adaedificat in coelo ascensionem suam.
Amos. Who builds his ascent in heaven.

13.*Philipp.* Inde venturus est judicare vivos et mortuos.
Philip. Who shall judge the quick and dead.

14.*Malachii.* Ascendam ad vos in judicio et ero vobis iesus.
Malachi. I will come to you in judgment and be a Saviour to you.

15.*Bartholomeus.* Credo in spiritum sanctum.

Bartholomew. I believe in the Holy Ghost.

16.*Joel.* Effundam de spiritu meo super omnem carnem.
Joel. I will pour out my spirit upon all flesh.

17.*Mattheus.* Sanctam ecclesiam catholicam sanctorum communionem.
Matthew. The holy catholic church, the communion of saints.

18.*Sophonias.* Invocabunt eum omnes et servent ei.
Zephaniah. They shall call upon and shall serve Him.

19.*Simon.* Remissionem peccatorum.
Simon. The remission of sins.

20.*Mychias.* Deponet dominus omnes iniquitates vestras.
Micah. The Lord shall take away all your iniquities.

The screen without doubt anciently extended across the south aisle and within there was an altar, as can be seen by referring to note 3 at the end of this chapter. By the removal of this part of the screen the creed is not finished; it would however be so by the addition of two panels, and thus the words

> *"Carnis resurrectionem"*
> Resurrection of the body
> *"Vitam aeternam. Amen."*
> And the life everlasting. *Amen.*

would render it complete.

On the north side of the chancel the before mentioned monument to Sir Pierce Courtenay is ornamented with pilasters, coats of arms, etc. On the top are the arms of the Courtenay family, with a *crescent* for difference, impaling those of Shilston. Above the pilaster, on the right side, are the arms of Clifford, with a *crescent charged with a mullet*, impaling those of Staplehill. Above the left pilaster are the arms of Clifford, with a *crescent charged with a mullet*, signifying that he was the third son of the second house. Below the centre coat of arms is the following inscription:

"*Sir Pierce Courtnay married Elizabeth ye daughter of Robert Shilston, who had issue VII children: Carew, Edward and James, sonns; also daughters Katharine, married to Kempthorn; Dorothy, married to Cowlinge; Anne, married to Clifford and Joan, married to Tremayne.*"

Then follows a Greek inscription signifying that this monument was erected by Thomas Clifford in memory of his ancesters.

Below the Greek:

"Ecclus.4. *Strive for the truth unto death, and defend justice for thy life, and the Lord God shall fighte for thee.*"

Beneath this inscription is the figure of a man in armour, in a kneeling posture at a desk, with a book open before him. Over his head are the arms of Courtenay painted on the wall.

"Psal.112. *She hath distributed, and given to the poore, her righteousness remayneth for ever.*"

Beneath this inscription is a figure of a woman in a kneeling posture at a desk, with a book open before her. Over her head are the arms of Shilston painted on the wall. Beneath, on an altar-stone, is the following inscription:

"*Here lieth the body of Sir Pierce Courtney, knight, sonne to S.r Wil:m Courtney of Powdra, knight, who died Ano: Do: 1552, May 20, and also the body of Dame Elizabeth his wife, sole daughter and heire to Robert Shilston of Bridstowe, Esquire, who died the 8th of*

No: Ano: Do: 1605."

Other tablets and ancient floor-stones are in the chancel, but these we leave to describe another conspicuous monument in the south aisle, to the *"memory of James Eastchurch"*, before referred to: his effigies as low as the waist, are fixed in a niche in the wall.[4] He is represented in the act of praying, a velvet cushion before him; his hair straightly combed on his forehead, a single curl round his neck and a large ruff; a black gown, full at the sleeves, and a crimson waistcoat. Under is the following inscription:

"Memoriae sacrum Jacobi Eastchurch parva corporis minore animi, imbecillitate, 85 feliciter complevit annos qui prolem habuit tres filios, Richardu Henr & Rober. Ut autem inter Angelos feliciorem agat.......apud Praedium suum Lawell Co D......Decemb.Ao Di 1631, libentr ob....."

> *"Blest pilgrime Eastchurch, long thou'st travell'd. and*
> *At length with joy attain'd the Holy Land.*
> *Thou'st left this militant and ta'en thy way*
> *To Heaven's triumphant church to live for aye;*
> *(As thy forefathers did) rest thou with them*
> *For ever in the New Jerusalem."*

On a black marble below:

"Secus hoc marmor recumbit corpus Jacobi Eastchurch de Lawell generosi die x Decembris sepultum Anno Domini, 1662."

"Also Shilston, the wife of James Eastchurch, gent. daughter of the Right Reverend & Worshipfull Thomas Clifford, doctor in divinitie, was buried the first day of March, 1685."

In the rural districts of England and Wales churchyards have ever claimed attention, and ever have been objects of great interest, and sometimes they contain the sole memorial of families long extinct. Few, if any, possess a site more beautiful than ours, occupying as it does the south-western extremity of the eminence on which the town stands; it is considerably elevated above the road, and with the church and tower presents a pleasing and conspicuous object. The trees that adorn the yard are of long standing and noble growth; upon them the rooks annually build their nests; their monotonous cawing well harmonises with the solemnity of the place. The fresh breezes that play over the green sward, and the picturesque views it commands, strikingly contrast with the confined burial places of our crowded cities. Some of the old inhabitants remember the ancient lich gateway through which the yard was formerly entered, as well as another entrance by a steep flight of steps immediately opposite the tower. There were also, before the fire, three old cottages built on the churchyard wall, their windows overlooking the yard, and thus destroying its calm and seclusive aspect. The present iron gates and handsome stone pillars are in good taste, and well accord with the recent alterations and improvements of the church. The boundary walls and ancient tombstones were lately re-erected and repaired, the uneven surface of the ground levelled and the paths newly arranged. The expenses of these various improvements were considerable and were defrayed by the benevolence of two liberal contributors to the principal charities of the town, independent of the sums raised for the repairs of the church.

From the external of the graveyard the mind involuntarily turns to death which so intimately concerns us all. It is a theme on which poets and moralists have expatiated in strains of tenderness, and to it the preacher alludes in words of deep pathos and earnest admonition. Here the great equaliser reigns and around us are the graves over which sorrowing relatives come and weep. It is a scene which solemnly impresses all, whether they confess it or not. Here the pinions of the gay droop — the uplifted head of the proud is lowered — the grasp of the covetous, and the stronghold of the avaricious are loosened – the energy that rivets our fond affections to earth is checked – the tide of life recedes – the prize becomes a blank – here the oppressed beholds a tyrant that conquers the oppressor – here the poor become rich if heirs of heaven, and without a hope beyond the grave the rich are poor indeed – mere bankrupts in the prospect of eternity. *"Here too the spirit is urged forward through the valley and shadow of death, and from the dark empire of the grave, onward to the everlasting future."* Though thus stern be the aspect of death and the grave, yet to the enlightened eyes of the Christian they are vanquished. The dust of countless generations are here held, but in a moment the trumpet shall sound and the dead shall be raised 'incorruptible'.

The tombstones are numerous but the limits of this work will only admit of our giving two or three of the most striking; as a whole they teach the oft repeated lesson that no age is exempt from death, his trophies are the young and robust as well as the old and infirm: *"who so artful as to put it by"*. On the first gravestone that claims attention, Robert Woolcombe is said to have been vicar of this parish sixty three years. He was instituted in 1600 and died 1654. This contradiction can be explained by it being known that he laboured as a curate to his father Benedict and the whole of his ministry was here included.

"Here lyeth the body of Robert Woolcombe, vicar of this church threescore and three years, who died the 19th day of January, 1654. And here resteth under hope of resurrection to eternal life."

The first three lines of the following poetical effusion were the production of two aspiring natives who were lost in their grand object, the praises of the departed, when they attempted a description of Haldon; however, a third came to their rescue and the last two lines gave a finished composition.

"Sacred to the memory of the Rev. Ambrose Wilkins, who departed this life the 15th day of May, 1774, in the 85th year of his age. Master of the Grammar-school in this parish."

> *"The dreary wild, the dreadful storm*
> *To him were trifling cares;*
> *Who did endure,*
> *Serv'd Ashcombe cure[5]*
> *For more than 50 years."*

This inscription to John Tothill on the south side of the churchyard is a touching composition. It is from the pen of Mr. Matthews, a solicitor of this place. Mr. Tothill was a self-taught philosopher, astronomer and mathematician of no ordinary merit. Although his talents led to no important results, yet they were highly esteemed, and his virtues were long cherished by a large circle of friends and relatives.

"Sacred to the memory of John Tothill, son of Nicholas and Ann Tothill of this parish, who died the 24th day of July 1760."

> *"Strangers or Friends, if learn'd or good, draw near,*
> *For such as you this tomb demands a tear;*
> *For lo! the dust inclosed was once endued*
> *With every talent to be wise and good.*
> *Learn'd, tho' untaught, in all that schools cou'd teach,*
> *That judgment could improve, or genius reach:*
> *Yet knew no pride, a soul above disguise,*
> *That nothing wish'd to be but good and wise:*
> *He liv'd a blessing on mankind bestow'd,*

And died at last an offering fit for God!"

The advowson of the parish of Chudleigh is in the gift of the parishioners who purchased it of John Hunt of Hams Barton on the 19th of April, 1683, for the sum of £160, (to be) taken from the parish chest. By a deed bearing the same date, the benefice was conveyed to certain persons in trust or confidence, requiring them to give on two several sabbaths, within four months after the avoidance of the vicarage, notice for a meeting of the parishioners holding lands rated at £5 per annum. At this meeting it was further ordered that the majority should choose and nominate their future vicar. Accordingly the first election took place on the 10th February, 1688, when Nicholas Battersby, as will be seen by the subjoined list of vicars, (taken from Dr. Oliver's Ecclesiastical History) was chosen and nominated.

The living of Chudleigh is valued at £550 per annum; when therefore (in times like the present) a vacancy occurs by the death or removal of the vicars of Chudleigh, and advertisements give publicity to the fact, it brings into the field a host of candidates. These have each an opportunity of preaching on the several sabbaths during the period of four months prior to the election. Their testimonials are also laid before the voters and the town at large for their careful perusal. Chudleigh is thus in possession of a privilege enjoyed but by few episcopal congregations in England, and which gives the parishioners (unless they unguardedly promise their votes) firstly, perfect freedom in the choice of their minister and, secondly, a great number to choose from. The judicious exercise of religious liberty, without any local influence whatever, was evidently the grand object that our pious ancestors contemplated and provided for when they made a considerable effort to purchase and place, at the entire disposal of the landed rate-payers, the advowson of the vicarage. The real value of what Chudleigh thus possesses can perhaps be better estimated and understood by a careful examination of the important religious movement that took place in Scotland in 1843.

The present trustees are Lord Exmouth, Sir Lawrence Palk, Major General Taylor, Mr. Parker, Major Fortescue and Mr. Burrington.

The following is the list of vicars before referred to:

Nicholas is the first name that I have met with, and I believe is the Vicar who bequeathed in 1303 to the Fabric of Exeter Cathedral vis.viii*d*.

John Fitz Hugh occurs Vicar the 29th September, 1317.

Nicholas Coffin, instituted the 20th June, 1337.

Thomas de Marston, the 23rd March, 1348.

Thomas Walsh ————: he exchanged for Axminster with

Richard de Hatheleseye, 23rd March, 1352.

Philip Bossayon, instituted the 14th July, 1353: he also exchanged for the Vicarage of Dunsford with

Robert Brugge, 28th March, 1387.

John Basyngham de Melton ————: he exchanged for Luppit with

Vincent Hille, the 22nd January, 1402. This Vicar resigning,

Ralph Colle succeeded, the 13th January, 1422.

N.B. *Colle* exchanged for Lustleigh with

John Burleigh, the 21st November, 1428.

Michael occurs Vicar the 14th February, 1449.

Stephen Colyn: ————on whose death

Edward Stephynson followed the 16th October, 1499.

N.B. He exchanged for a Prebend in St. Probus' Cornwall, with

Edward Carr (alias *George*) the 23rd July, 1505

Robert Weston: ———— on whose resignation

Ralph Holland, instituted the 18th September, 1508.

Stephen Vernay, on Holland's resignation, the 27th June, 1516.

William Leveson: ———

N.B. King Henry VIII in his Writ to Bishop Veysey, dated the 20th July, 1536, required of his Lordship, under a Penalty of £500, a return of the value of all ecclesiastical preferments in the Diocese of Exeter, with the names of every incumbent from the 1st January, 1535, the said Valuation to be delivered in the Court of Chancery under the Episcopal Seal by 3rd November, 1536. In this Valuation I read:

"Vicaria de Chudleigh, ubi Willelmus Leveson est Vicarius, valet £xxi."

John Blaxton succeeded on Leveson's resignation.

George Chudleigh collated the 27th August, 1541; he was made a Canon of Exeter Cathedral, the 9th March, 1546.

John More, ——— 1559.

Benedict Woolcombe the 16th January, 1571. His will dated the 4th October, 1599, was proved the 25th January following. (Patroness, Christina Chudleigh.)

Robert Woolcombe, son of Benedict, the 18th January, 1600, *Patrons hac vice* William Putt, James and Thomas Eastchurch. This Vicar died on the 19th January, 1654.

Stephen Bloy, May 10th, 1658, on whose death

Edward Northmore succeeded the 30th December, 1673, Patron John Hunt, Gent. Mr. Northmore died the 2nd October, 1687.

Nicholas Battersby, the 10th February following, on the presentation of John Coysh, John Cholwich, Giles Inglett, Christopher Hellier, John Langley and James Rennell, Trustees of the Advowson.

John Ellis, on Battersby's death, admitted the 4th January, 1689. Presented by six Trustees: ob. 2nd March, 1709, aet., 63.

Nicholas Tripe, admitted the 30th June, 1710. Patrons as before.

John Sergeant, admitted on Tripe's death, the 16th October, 1718.

John Bayly, admitted on Sergeant's death, the 12th June, 1736. Patrons as before.

William Staplin, admitted on Bayly's death, 10th September, 1751. Patrons as before.

Gilbert Burrington, admitted on Staplin's death, 12th June, 1752. Patrons as before. This worthy Vicar died 23rd February, 1785, aet. 63.

Gilbert Burrington, admitted on his father's death, 28th June, 1785. Patrons as before.

Wilmot Henry Palk, admitted on Burrington's death, 24th June, 1841. Presented by the Trustees.

The Presbyterian Chapel was founded in 1710. There were formerly connected with it some of the most wealthy and influential inhabitants of the parish; one of these, Mr. Causley of Ranscombe, endowed it with £20 per annum which is still paid out of some land purchased by the late Lord Clifford, subject to this annual payment. The last of the Presbyterian ministers was the Rev. B. Peckford, a learned man and profound Hebrew scholar. After the fire the chapel was for some years without a settled minister. Being difficult to obtain one from among the Presbyterians, it was thought advisable to apply to Mr. Wilson, a wealthy patron of the Independent academy at Hoxton; he accordingly sent a popular preacher, the Rev. James Davison. On his resignation, a succession of the same denomination continuing to serve this church, it was finally changed from Presbyterian to Independent. In 1830 this chapel was rebuilt on a larger scale under the direction of the Rev. J. Allen[6], the present minister, and with consent of the trustees; It will seat about 350. There have at different periods been added a vestry, schoolrooms and burying ground; there is also belonging to it a Sunday School (the first established in the town), a girl's day school and vestry library. It contains a fine and powerful organ, the gift of the late benevolent Mrs. Davison, to whose memory and her excellent partner, there is on the north wall a neat tablet, as also near the pulpit another to Mr. Petherick and grandson; the inscriptions are as follows:

"Beneath are deposited the mortal remains of James Davison, Minister of the gospel in this place, who departed this life to be with Christ, August 5th, 1841. Also of Elizabeth, his wife, who fell asleep in Jesus, March 6th, 1847."

> *"Peace be within this sacred place,*
> *And joy a constant guest!*
> *With holy gifts and heavenly grace,*
> *Be her attendants blest."*

"In this chapel are deposited the mortal remains of John Petherick, who died the 12th June, 1836, aged 55 years. Also John P. Allen, grandson of the above, ob. 17th Jan., 1834. Aet. 5 years and 6 mo."

> *"Cease, friendship, cease to weep!*
> *God takes but what he gives;*
> *And while the relics sleep,*
> *The immortal spirit lives.*
> *Mourner retire, and kiss the afflictive rod,*
> *To thee their exit calls,*
> *'Prepare to meet thy God."*

The Wesleyan Chapel, situated in Mill Lane, was built in 1837. It belongs to the Teignmouth circuit and is regularly supplied by the ministers and local preachers on the Conference plan. The scriptural doctrines and form of church government of the Wesleyan Methodists are well known.

Brookfield Chapel, or the United Christian Church of the Baptist persuasion, was erected near this town in 1850 by the generous efforts of W. Rouse, Esq. It is a neat and commodious building and presents a substantial and plain elevation; the interior is marked by the same regard to simplicity and comfort, the pulpit is a model of neatness, constructed, as also the seats, of a kind of wood lately introduced into this country from New Zealand. There belongs to it a large and flourishing Sabbath-school. The burying ground adjoins the chapel. The baptistery is at the residence of W. Rouse, Esq., who fills the pastoral office to this church. Boys, girls and infant day-schools are supported by the same generous individual, their duties being sustained by trained superintendents on the 'British System' under the able inspection of Mrs. Rouse.

The various gifts to the poor which when bestowed were considerable, are from the relative value of money and other causes at present but of trifling consideration. The parish lands and tenements have been leased out on long terms, and are scarcely worth enumerating.[7] We also find in the report of the Commissioners that there were many charities once belonging to the parish under the head of 'Lost Gifts'. Of the annual annuities, the following are the principal:

By Sir John Acland in bread, fifty-two shillings. It is not bestowed weekly according to the donor's direction, but is given together with Clarke's gift every quarter, when a baker is directed to furnish forty sixpenny loaves. The tickets for the disposal of this bread are at the discretion of the churchwardens. The distribution at the Easter quarter is greater by four loaves in order to exhaust the whole sum of four pounds two shillings. Clarke's gift is paid out of two closes of land called Reeve Oaks and Veversham, in the parish of Trusham.

Soper's gift pays forty shillings per annum out of houses near the church, which the parish leased out on a long term of years. This gift was to be laid out in the purchase of linen cloth for shirting, which was ordered to be given away by the churchwardens, *"to such poor labourers of the parish as have poor families, each individual receiving sufficient to make a shirt"*. When the report of the charities was published the churchwardens were enabled to supply ten poor labourers annually.

William Stidson, Esquire, who died the 13th April, 1818, gave £100 to the poor of the parish for ever; the interest, £4 per annum, to be laid out half-yearly in bread at the discretion of the churchwardens for the use and benefit of the poor and industrious not receiving alms.

Stephen Bloy by will bearing date the 11th June, 1672, gave to the poor of the parish of Chudleigh £25 to remain as a stock, the interest of which being yearly thirty shillings, one half to be distributed to such persons as should be in sickness; preferring the most religious and sober, as well as had no relief from the parish; to be given in sums not exceeding three shillings to any in one or the same sickness. The other half was to be distributed to poor passengers and travellers in distress. This gift of Stephen Bloy was included in a sum of £140, with which the old workhouse was purchased by the parish of Nicholas Stuckie of Ashcombe in the year 1675.

The workhouse was rebuilt by the parish (as before stated) and finally repurchased by Mr. Williams,[8] subject to this annuity of thirty shillings per annum. It is necessary while on the charities to correct an error made by the writer in the preceding ancient history referring to the fairs and markets. The different amounts mentioned in the parish records were paid to Hunt on account of Thomas Bridges, as the following short extract will show: *"By indenture bearing date the first of May, one thousand five hundred and ninety-seven, between Thomas Bridges on one part and Henry Clifford and twenty-two, on the other part; for the consideration of one hundred and fifty pounds:*

the market and fairs as also a sporting or playing place then estimated at three acres, should ever remain for the use of the said parish".

Among the charities enumerated by the Commissioners we find the churchhouse, the upper part of which has for centuries been used as a parish schoolroom. It is the most ancient educational building in the town and is mentioned in a deed bearing date 1597, where it is included with other parish lands held in trust. The masters have of late years been elected at a general vestry meeting, and are permitted to occupy the premises rent free, as also the sexton who resides under the same roof. The first notice concerning this school in the parochial register refers to the year 1605 and again in 1657 when 'the seven men' and the parishioners at a meeting held for the purpose took into consideration *"the great want of an able paynful school master and agreed with one Mr. Pollexfen to come to keepe school here in Chudleigh. They promised to give him thirteen pounds six shillings and eightpence for the first year, and to repayer the schoolhouse and chamber adjoining in convenyent manner".* Mr. Pollexfen on his part promised to be very careful and diligent in teaching those scholars which should be sent to him, and for the consideration aforesaid, to *"teach and instruct in the best manner he could six poor men's children of the psh.; such as the seven or any five of them should appoint".* The masters of late years have in addition to the day-school admitted boarders.

At the time that Mr. Bond filled the important office this school became one of the best of the description in the county. He was a clever and practical arithmetician and good astronomer for his day; he had a most pleasing method of imparting knowledge. His mild and amiable temper greatly endeared him to his numerous pupils, many of whom were in after life distinguished for their abilities in their various callings, ever recollecting their youthful sojourn here with much delight. To Mr. Bond is the town indebted for the erection of several commodious and respectable houses.

Mr. George Flood, the present estimable master of the school, teaches nine children, who are appointed by the minister and churchwardens, in reading, writing and arithmetic, under Eastchurch's gift, which after deducting the land tax amounts to £4 12s. 6d. per annum. This gift is paid out of Chatteshall or Catshole, now the property of Sir Lawrence Palk. The will of Richard Eastchurch, the donor of this charity, bears the date the 14th March, 1692. One half of this yearly bequest was to have been expended in bibles and good books, and the other half to such person or persons as should diligently teach four poor children to read and write. Of late years it has been thought advisable to devote the whole to education.

The Free Grammar School is the principal charity of the town and was founded by John Pynsent, Esquire, who was born and educated in Chudleigh. On a tablet in front of the old schoolhouse is the following inscription: *"John Pynsent, of Lincolns Inn, Esquire, born in this parish, hath erected this for a Free School, and endowed it with thirty pounds per annum for ever, one thousand six hundred and sixty-eight"*. In consideration of £8.00 paid to 'the seven men', an acre of ground taken from the play-park was conveyed to him and he agreed with them *"at his costs, to build a house thereupon for keeping a school, and for the habitation of a master, and to enclose the rest of the ground with a wall for a garden and orchard"*. Mr. Pynsent died on the 29th August, 1668, before the schoolhouse was completed, and although he left sufficient property to defray all legacies and charitable bequests, yet so backward were his Executors in fulfilling the requirements of his will that an application in consequence was made to the Court of Chancery, and after a full investigation of the affair it was decreed that the schoolhouse should be completed, a master appointed and a salary of £30 per annum be paid to him half-yearly, free from all deductions, out of his estate at Combe in the parish of Croydon, Surrey. The school was to be free for the inhabitants of Chudleigh and to be called 'Pynsent's Free School'. Sir Thomas Clifford was one of the trustees then appointed, their full number being eleven. The majority have the power to elect a master. Mr. Pynsent directed that the schoolmaster should be of good name, manners and teaching, and conformable to the doctrines and discipline of the Church of England. For a short time after the death of the founder some exhibitions appear to have been attached to the school. According to the Commissioners account of this charity he gave £100 for apprenticing twenty poor children of Croydon and Chudleigh, and to each of them that could read a bible, also to five poor boys of Chudleigh £3.00 each yearly, for five years, towards buying books and clothes, and to be taught at the 'Free School' in Chudleigh; but he directed that this exhibition should cease to such of the said boys as should not diligently attend their schooling, and frequent the church every Lord's day; and to three of the said boys that should be thought fit for the university, he gave £5.00 each, for four years, for their maintenance at the University of Cambridge.

It does not appear that there was any fund granted for the continuance of these exhibitions, nor any regulations for the future appointment of more boys to succeed the three chosen by his executors. Had Mr. Pynsent lived there is every reason to suppose that this 'Free School' would have been made by him a superior establishment. From the salary being left in money instead of land, it has not augmented. The entire cessation of the exhibitions was doubtless also a great disadvantage to the prosperity of the foundation and the advancement of the pupils by depriving them of that emulation which, when once aroused, impels the ardour of youth onward through the by no means royal road to the acquirement of knowledge. However, no such inducement can now be held out and the original intentions of the founder in reference to his native place do not appear to have met with the success he intended, for comparatively few of the children of the town or parish are educated in this 'Free Grammar School'. However, as a classical boarding school, it has at different periods attained considerable celebrity. It is at present in high repute, having steadily increased after the election of the Rev. C.M. Edward Collins to the mastership, on whose resignation two years since, it was presented to the Rev. George Moyle, and is still advancing in the estimation of the public.

Among the many excellent clergymen who have from time to time been elected to fill the situation of headmaster to this school (as a native of the town), we would notice the Rev. William Pulling, who however filled the important office but for a short period, preferring his literary circle of friends in the University of Cambridge, where he has distinguished himself as a linguist of no ordinary merit. His lectures on the derivation and classification of the various modern languages were highly approved of by men of eminence in that important branch of learning. Mr. Pulling published a translation of sermons from the Danish and is the author of a volume of sonnets, dedicated to the Duke of Wellington; he is now the rector of Dymchurch, Kent where he resides.

Invalids will find in Chudleigh a variety of excellent accommodation in the way of lodgings and houses. The Clifford Arms for many years (prior to the opening of the South Devon Railway) kept by Mr. Petherick in the best possible style, is still open and occupied by its proprietor, Mrs. Cartwright. Here families can obtain board and lodging on a large scale, as the apartments belonging to this spacious house are most commodious and convenient.

There are also many excellent shops of every description which are well stocked with goods, thus enabling the inhabitants and visitors to obtain an immediate supply of all they may require.

The Chudleigh Literary Society, instituted in 1848, has in connection with it a Reading-Room well supplied with daily and other papers, and an increasing Library. Lectures on different subjects are delivered by the members of the society, as well as by others who are occasionally engaged for the general benefit of the town.

1. From the Gaelic word Tain, water or stream.

2. There is an entry in the parish records, *"paid for taking down the altar stone"*, in the year 1568; *"paid for making of the timber work about the newe commandements"*, in 1578; and also *"paid the painter for making of the X.commandements"*: it further appeareth that the functionaries were very slow in executing the commands issued by the Lord Bishop, for they were cited to appear in court in 1579 by the following item: *"paid for that defaulte was found for lack of the Tenne Commandements and other things in the church; paid charges of appearing before the Lord Bishop in visitation; paid the sumler (sumner) that assyted (cited) us to appear; paid charges when we brought in our answers at the visitation; paid ffees of the court"*.

3. In the south aisle stood formerly the altar of the Virgin Mary, before which Thomas Taylor, a canon of Crediton Church, desired by his last will and testament to be buried. For the use of the said altar he bequeathed a silver chalice. The will, proved the 15th December, 1452, may be seen in Bishop Lacy's register.

4. In the wall where this monument is fixed there are the remains of the stone steps that led to the rood-loft; the portion of the screen that is deficient was no doubt taken down when it was removed.

5. It may be curious to some of our readers to remark the singularity of the above epitaph in honor of this old 'gymnasiarch', so styled by Dr. Fraser Halle; it becomes doubly interesting when we call to mind that our present vicar whose residence is at Ashcombe, has the same journey to perform; we cannot but rejoice that although the wilds of Haldon are alike dreary, yet 'dreadful storms' have no longer to be encountered, the winters having become more like the mild close of autumn than the deep snowy seasons of past ages.

6. The Rev. J. Allen is the author of the Daily Monitor and Daily Companion in two vols., which have passed through several editions.

7. The whole amount raised from parish lands (market excepted) is £10 13s. 8d. per annum. When the present leases have expired, they will return about £80, according to the calculation of the Commissioners.

8. This building has been converted into a National school and contains spacious boy's, girl's and infant schoolrooms, with a committee room, and accommodation for the residence of the female teacher. The alteration was made at the sole expense of Mr. Williams, who keeps the entire building in repair, and presents it to the school committee free from any expense whatever. Such liberality needs no comment.

CHAPTER VI

The extensive domain of Ugbrooke, as it regards its own exquisite scenery, and the prominent part it takes in that of Chudleigh, deserves a pen far better skilled in the art of description than the writer's. It is situated about a mile east of the town and occupies, in conjunction with some well cultivated farms, a vale of considerable extent. The park itself covers an area of 600 acres and is stocked with about the same number of deer. Enclosed on all sides save one (towards the South Hams) by its own richly clothed eminences, it takes no aid from surrounding prospects until the heights that thus encircle it are ascended; the rural and varied charms which distinguish it are therefore its own.

Ugbrooke before possessed by the present noble family, was no doubt in a comparatively rude and uncultivated state, with every capability by its mild temperature and peculiar undulations, of rising under the plastick hand of man, into a region of calm seclusion not to be easily surpassed. The stream from which its name was derived is no longer characteristic of the Saxon wog broca, 'crooked brook', as by expansion, it altogether conceals its rude and winding channel and now forms three small lakes. These are altogether free from symmetrical formality, too often the accompaniment of such artificial adornments; on the contrary they are here truly beautiful.

The first adjoins the Ashwell gate, now one of the principal approaches to the house; it has been considerably enlarged and improved by the present Baron, lying beneath a high and thickly wooded bank, the mansion is completely hidden though so near. This expanse of water with its rustic boathouse, has a wild and seclusive aspect, and leaves the mind unprepared for the many different attractions that cluster round the one always designated the pond, which is skirted on the east by the lovely and verdant lawn on which the house stands; beyond are eminences gently rising, adorned with trees of great beauty. On the west are presented to the view undulations of more abrupt and varied character, which unite with the woody heights that form the boundary that separates the park from the Chudleigh vale. The banks that immediately skirt the pond are planted with white and red hawthorn interspersed with chestnuts and other trees that overhang and dip their graceful branches into its placid surface. This placidity is only comparative, from the current through the vale, it is generally agitated by a gentle ripple that gives a pleasing animation to the scene. Visitors are accommodated with a seat under a noble oak at the edge of the water. This vividly reflects the house, library and chapel, thus giving a double image of their unpretending beauty. The features of this landscape are peculiarly harmonious and sylvan, and cannot but fill the mind with the calm enjoyment such scenes are calculated to inspire. Within a few paces of this seat on the right there rises a mass of lime rock with an old quarry and kiln concealed by trees, and fringed by the forked roots of others partly laid bare by the excavations beneath: these still flourish in leafy verdure with each returning spring. Beneath this rock wells up a spring of water clear as crystal, called Pit Well, which, after flowing on calmly a little way, dashes over a bank where some stones are placed so as to form a cascade.

Immediately below is the third and last expanse of water, called the lower pond. This like the first is rude and sequestered; at its termination a decoy has been made for wild fowl. The Ugg here resumes its natural and diminished course, and flowing a little below the hamlet of Gappah, at a distance of about two miles, is lost in the Teign. Belonging to this park are numerous roads skirting the water or winding through the extensive plantations of limes, chestnuts and a rich variety of flowering shrubs.

On the Newton turnpike road is situated the grand triple avenue. In the height of summer it uprears its gothic arches of grateful shade repelling every ray of the sun's fierce heat. This avenue is constituted triple by presenting as entered through a handsome gateway, two side avenues that run parallel with the Newton Road. In addition to the rock already described, there are other masses jutting up amid the trees; these are adorned with flowers and festooned with the wild bramble and ivy, beautifully contrasting with the smooth and verdant pastures around. The perfection to which this park has arrived has been the gradual development in the luxuriant growth of timber or forest trees; they are of all descriptions and worthy more than a passing notice, if the limits of this sketch did not forbid their being particularised; some of them are immense, being the growth of centuries. Prince, who lived in the time of the second Baron, mentions his planting chestnuts and other trees extensively. The grand masses of oaks and groups of beech are of still more ancient growth, and may be considered as indigenous. Although time has worn out the strength of many, they are still beautiful in old age and decay. The woods say Polwhele *"sweep wildly round, pursuing the course of the valley, presenting the finest features of extensive lawn, smooth and verdant"*, between groups of trees, others again appear: *"The same object assumes a different aspect by a successive change of view."*

On the high ground towards Chudleigh is the Danish circular encampment before mentioned. It is formed by a deep trench, in some places double. The trees with which it has from time to time been planted must have tended greatly to its preservation. The walk through the encampment on the brow of the hill is rich in prospect; on the one hand, the finest features of the park, noble eminences 'with their magnificent masses of shadow'; on the other, the Chudleigh vale with its cheerful town, noble rock, and all the attractions that encircle it.

This landscape cannot be well surpassed. The park on the southern extremity is closed in by thick plantations of fine trees. The vale terminates in a barren tract of country called the sands, which with about fifteen acres of the park, are in the adjoining parish of Kingsteignton.

After the death of the Lord Treasurer in 1673 the family secluded themselves at Ugbrooke, far away from the stormy arena of politics, the Test Act having severed them from offices and emoluments; unless when called to the battlefield for their country's good. The extension and adornment of this their noble park claimed their constant and undivided attention. Several of the representatives of this family possessed enthusiasm in a religion, distinguished by a sensitive attention to the effect of externals on the mind; they were also evidently close observers as well as warm admirers of nature.

Roman Catholics, however vast their undertakings in buildings, or the laying out of parks or gardens, seldom err or do violence to the simple but little understood element of refined taste. The embellishments of Ugbrooke are in perfect accordance with nature, its various undulations are clothed as they should be, to form an endless variety, and the variety, a grand whole.

A grove in the park towards the Newton Road, known as Dryden's Walk, is pointed out as having been a favourite resort of this great man on his visits to the Lord Treasurer, his friend and patron. One year only was the difference in the respective ages of these extraordinary public characters. They were also alike tossed about by the fierce and uncertain political and religious events of the period in which they lived. After the death of the Lord Treasurer a warm friendship arose between the poet and Hugh, the second Baron, the youthful son of his lamented friend. Dryden's visits to Ugbrooke appear to have continued to the end of his days and, if tradition be correct, he there completed his translation of Virgil. His many solitary pacings to and fro beneath the deep shade of the beechen groves, united to the wild and romantic scenery which the park then presented, could not but have been favourable to those flights of imagination, and have also tended to kindle those poetic raptures, the force and harmony of which have been seldom equalled. The subject of the Eclogues was also somewhat in accordance with the rural character of all around.

The dedication to Dryden's translation of the Pastorals (of which a short extract is given) was addressed to Lord Clifford. It is a specimen of the laudatory style of such compositions in an age when poetic genius, that has never been surpassed, had to obtain by flattery the patronage of the great. The praise here bestowed was doubtless sincere and well merited and can therefore be read with pleasure.

"My Lord, I know to whom I dedicate: and could not have been induced by any motive, to put this part of Virgil, or any other into unlearned hands. You have read him with pleasure, and I daresay with admiration, in the Latin, of which you are a master. You have added to your natural endowments which, without flattery, are eminent, the superstructures of study, and the knowledge of good authors. Courage, probity and humanity are inherent in you. These virtues have ever been habitual to the ancient House of Cumberland from whence you are descended."

And again, as though the poet felt keenly his noble friend's separation by the Test Act from a life of political importance and activity, he adds: *"rural recreations abroad, and books at home, are the innocent pleasures of a man who is early wise; and gives fortune no more hold of him, than of necessity he must. It is good, on some occasions, to think beforehand as little as we can; to enjoy as much of the present as will not endanger our futurity, and to provide ourselves with the virtuoso's saddle, which will be sure to amble when the world is upon the hardest trot".*

Before bringing the description of the park to a close, we may remark that the ponds are well stocked with fine carp, dace, perch, pike, eel and trout. The rabbit warrens contain an unlimited number of these little animals and they afford no small amusement to the visitors as they are seen on the approach of footsteps darting to their countless holes; while the herds of deer if disturbed bound across the eminences or dash through the water with swiftness, elegance and grace that must greatly delight the beholder.

Having described the park, we next proceed to give some account of the house, as also a few particulars relative to the succession of the different Barons, as given by Dr. Oliver in his *Cliffordiana*. The house when occupied by the Precentors before the Reformation was doubtless a dull and inconvenient abode,[1] for we read of no important improvements effected on it until the time of the Lord Treasurer when, besides the chapel, he began the erection of a new mansion, leaving £2000 at his death for its completion. The peerage and estates came to his eldest surviving son, Hugh, in his tenth year. He possessed the title fifty seven years and well supported the character of a benevolent, hospitable and patriotic English nobleman. The park and its plantations claimed his principal attention. He married in the year 1685 Ann, the daughter of Sir Thomas Preston of Furness, in the county of Lancashire, Bart. This lady brought him considerable property in Warwickshire, Derbyshire, Lancashire and Westmoreland. By her he had issue nine sons and six daughters.

The third Baron of Chudleigh was the seventh son. He married Elizabeth Blount, who brought him a fortune of £4000 paid at the marriage and £2000 more on the decease of her mother. His father was violently opposed to his marriage, but may have altered his opinion when he saw the Duke of Norfolk united to his sister. During the short period that he possessed the peerage nothing memorable is recorded of him. He died in 1732.

Hugh, fourth Baron, was born Michaelmas Day, 1726. He married Lady Ann Lee, fifth daughter of George Henry Lee, second Earl of Lichfield, by whom he had eight children. To his nobleman are his family indebted for the erection of the present house. The former mansion projected by Lord Treasurer was by all accounts a long straggling and inconvenient habitation. After mature consideration as to whether he was able to complete the building without injury to his fortune and family, he began the work by pulling down a part of the old house about 1760. The fabric gradually advanced under the direction of the celebrated Adam. By a judicious system of economy he was prepared at the end of a few years to remove into a comfortable and well proportioned dwelling. His principle was *"pay as you go"*; he was firmly convinced that nothing can be honorable that is not strictly just. Of all men he was the most punctual in acting up to the full extent of every obligation. Reverenced, honoured and beloved, he died peaceably in the arms of his family in 1783, recommending to them with his last breath concord and mutual affection.

In Hugh, the fifth Lord, were combined extraordinary beauty of person and fascinating urbanity of manners. In 1780 he married Appollonia, daughter and co-heiress of Marmaduke, the fifth Lord Langdale, but left no issue. After a long and lingering illness he expired in the bloom of life in 1793.

Charles, sixth Lord Clifford, was born in Jermyn Street, London on the 28th November, 1759, and was educated partly in the colleges of Donay, St. Omer's, Bruges and Liege. He married the daughter of Henry, the eighth Lord Arundell, by whom he had a large family. He succeeded to the title and estates the 15th January, 1793; he was distinguished by his warm patronage of the Arts, and everything connected with literature and philosophy, as also by the prominent part he took in the county business, and also in the training of the volunteers, which was considered an important and useful work during the long war. His services were highly appreciated and fully portrayed on a piece of plate presented by his lordship in 1802 by the commanding officers of the Yeomanry and Volunteer Corps.

The present Lord Hugh Charles was born in 1790 and married Mary Lucy Weld, only daughter of Cardinal Weld of Lulworth; he succeeded to the title in 1831. Lord Clifford has issue six sons and two daughters. Six only survive. Lady Clifford died in Rome on 15th May, 1831 where she was interred.

Ugbrooke House is an extensive modern structure, distinguished by great simplicity; quadrangular in form, with four turrets, and the whole finished with battlements. There is however one deviation from this form, which is a distinct wing, composed of the library and chapel, in a line with which there are (in the back area) a few remnants of the old house, a striking contrast with the present mansion. Though the site of the house may appear low when compared with the neighbouring elevations, yet in reality it commands fine views of the splendid scenery around, and is situated very dry and pleasant. The annexed list of paintings, with their respective positions, will convey some general idea of the principal suite of apartments, which are remarkable for their simple elegance and comfort.

The library may be considered one of the most delightful rooms in the building, and has an internal communication with the chapel which (as before stated) was built by the Lord Treasurer and, although improved at different periods, it was left for the present Baron to add considerably to its size and adornment. All these improvements have been conceived and executed in good taste: as a whole it presents a solemn and hallowed simplicity in this age of church decoration, and no description can convey an adequate idea of its beauty. The form of the building is oblong and lighted from windows situated in the vaulted roof. In the centre is suspended a lamp which, as in other Catholic chapels, is always kept burning: here amid the light of day it sheds a clear and extraordinary radiance which arises from the position of the windows. The altar piece, to which are attached the usual decorations, is very handsome; it occupies the upper end of the chapel, which is semi-circular. The walls of the sanctuary are cased with polished marble and in its centre is a painting representing the resurrection. On either side there are marble niches containing full length statues of Joseph and Mary. The pulpit occupies a recess in the wall and can be wound out and in at pleasure. Opposite is a similar seat, perhaps intended for a bishop or other dignitary. There are two side galleries facing each other; one contains a fine organ of powerful tone, the other gallery or tribune is occasionally used by visitors, and have their fronts decorated with 'basso-relievos'. The subjects they represent are Adam and Eve driven out of Paradise, the shepherds worshipping in the stable at Bethlehem, Christ at his daily occupation and the angels attending Christ. The tribune at the end for the accommodation of the family, in which are several busts, communicates with the library. The body of the chapel is furnished with seats that reach from the aisle under the side galleries. In addition to the main entrance to the chapel from the park, there are many others communicating with the pleasure garden and premises, thus rendering it accessible to the family in every direction. The mural tablets that were in the chapel to the memory of the Lord Treasurer and the fourth Baron have been removed, but are to be replaced.

The baptismal font, which is of marble, occupies an extremely small and quite a distinct apartment, the walls of which are covered with polished calcarious spar from Chudleigh rock. Pieces of sculpture representing the baptism of Christ, and an angel with a child, stand in an elevated position, between which and the font are vases filled with artificial flowers. Underneath the chapel is the burying place of the family; this is a neat arched apartment with a chequered marble floor, and contains a fine piece of statuary 'the three women at the foot of the cross', in front of which are two candelabras that when lighted show the tablets around on which are various inscriptions. The most conspicuous is one erected by the present Lord to the memory of his two infant children.

The pleasure gardens adjoining the house are spacious and kept in excellent order; they are filled with choice trees, shrubs, flowers and fountains.

DESCRIPTION OF THE PICTURES

Ferdinand II, Grand Duke of Tuscany, and an intimate friend of the Lord Treasurer Clifford, was, I believe, the donor of the choicest pictures in the Ugbrooke collection. Formerly this collection was much more considerable than at present; about thirty perished in the flames which consumed Mr. Anderson's premises in Covent Garden, London. Many of these I take to have been the Hunting Pieces mentioned by Evelyn in his memoirs, p.438, vol.1. *"18th Aug. 1673. My Lord Clifford being about this time returned from Tunbridge, and preparing for Devonshire, I went to take my leave of him at Wallingford House; he was packing up pictures, most of which were hunting wild beasts, and vast pieces of bull-baiting, bear-baiting, &c., &c."*.

HALL

1. *Charles, 6th Lord Clifford*, in the uniform of the Yeomanry. *Ramsey.*

2 & 3. *Colonel Taylor* and *J. Beaumont Swete, Esq.* Also in uniform. *Ramsey.*

4. *Lord Ebrington* now Earl Fortescue. *Ramsey.*

5. *Sir Thomas Ackland. Ramsey.*

6. *Hugh Charles, the present Lord Clifford. Ramsey.*

DINING ROOM

1. Sir Thomas Clifford (afterwards Lord Treasurer) as Comptroller of King Charles II's Household. This eminent statesman died at Ugbrooke 17th Oct. 1673, O.S. and was buried two days after in his chapel vault. The picture must have been painted about the year 1667, by *Sir Peter Lely.* N.B. Sir P. Lely died in 1680, aged 63.

2. A Farm Yard near Antwerp. The painter's name "*John Sibericks* 1661" is legible on the cart. This great Flemish painter died in 1703, aged 78. In the Journals of the Lords, 20th March, 1679 we read *"Ordered that John Siberchts, a Dutchman and Limner of Pictures, who, being a papist, ought to remove out of the cities of London and Westminster, may have liberty to stay in town for some time for the recovery of some debts owing to him before his removal out of this kingdom."* N.B. Six months were allowed him.

3. Elizabeth, daughter and co-heiress of William Martyn of Lindridge, Esq., and wife of the above-mentioned Sir Thos. Clifford. Her Ladyship died at Ugbrooke 21st Sept. 1709, and lies in the chapel vault near her husband. Painter *Sir Peter Lely.*

4. Catharine of Portugal, married to K. Charles II in May 1662. She remained in England about 30 years, and returning to Lisbon, died there 31st Dec. 1705, aged 67. *Sir P. Lely* has given her the characteristic emblems of *St. Catharine of Alexandria*, the wheel and palm.

5. *James, Duke of York*, afterwards K. James II. This unfortunate Prince and Sovereign died at St. Germaine, near Paris, 16th Sept. 1701, aged 68. *Sir P. Lely.*

6. *Her R.H. Anne, Duchess of York*, and lst wife of James above-mentioned. She was daughter to Edw. Hyde, Earl of Clarendon. Dying March 31st, 1671, aged 34, her Highness was interred in Westminster Abbey. *Sir P. Lely.*

7. *K. Charles II,* in his State Robes. Died Feb. 6th, 1685, aged 53. *Sir P. Lely.*

8. *Hugh, 2nd Lord Clifford*, Baron of Chudleigh, in a Court Dress.

9. *Fruit and Fish Piece.* On the rim of the Table we read "*I.B. Schonier* 1628".

10. *Thomas, eldest son of the Lord Treasurer Clifford.* He died at Florence, March 29th, 1671, aged 19, and his remains were brought over in an English frigate and deposited in the Ugbrooke vault July 28th that year. *Sir P. Lely.*

DRAWING ROOM

1. *Rev. Thomas Clifford, D.D.,* Grandfather of the Lord Treasurer. *Cornelius Jansens.*

2. *The Woman taken in Adultery*, 8th chapter of St. John. *Titian,* died 1576, aged 99.

3. *St. Mary of Egypt,* an illustrious penitent of the 5th century. By *Titian* also.

4. *Virgin and Child. Rubens.* This great painter died at Antwerp in 1640, aged 63.

5. *Christ blessing little children.* Mark, 10ch. 16v. The inscription is "*Peter Van Lint,* 1643".

6. *Christ presented by Pilate to the Multitude.* John, 19ch. 5v. A

coarse specimen of the low Dutch School.

7. *St. Mary Magdalene. Guido Rheni:* he died at Bologna 1642, aged 67.

8. *Tribute Money.* 24th ch. Mat. *Sir Anthony Vandyke,* who died in London 1641, aged 42.

9. *Holy Family,* by *Gentileschi.* Died 1647, aged 84. For an account of this picture see p.247 of Pilkington's "Lives of Painters".

10. *Lord Treasurer Clifford in his Study. Sir P. Lely.*

ANTI-ROOM

1. *Valley of Ice in Switzerland.* By *Francis Towne* of London. Died July 17th, 1816, aged 76, and buried in Heavitree Church.

2. *Hugh, 5th Lord Clifford*, who died at Munich, Jan. 15th, 1793, aged 37. By *Downman*, 1780.

3. & 4. Highly finished *Drawings* by *Payne,* in 1802.

5. *The late Lady Clifford and her Sister* (Mother to the late Lord Arundell) when children.

6 . *Hugh, 4th Lord Clifford,* who died Sept. 1st, 1783, aged 57. *Downman* 1781.

7. *Tivoli and Metellus' Tomb,* by *Ducroc.*

8. *Appollonia, 5th Lady Clifford.* Died Dec. 31st, 1815, aged 60, and lies at Hazlewood. *Downman.*

SECOND DRAWING ROOM

1. Over the fireplace, *Anne, 4th Lady Clifford*, and Mother to the late Charles, Lord Clifford. *Miss Reid.*

2. *Chudleigh Lime Rock,* by *Varley.* 1810.

3. *A Drawing* by *Prout.*

4. *View of the Simplon,* by *Nicholson.*

5. *View of Snowdon,* by *Varley.*

STATE BEDROOM

This Miracle of Art was finished from the designs and under the direction of Mary (Blount) who married Edward, 9th Duke of Norfolk, on 6th Nov. 1727. Her Grace intended it as a present for her nephew, Edward Howard, but on his untimely death she gave it to her other nephew, Hugh, the 4th Lord Clifford. This bed is beautifully described in the poem of Ugbrooke Park. A considerable part of the bed was destroyed in the dreadful fire at Worksop Manor in Oct. 1761. The damage on that occasion was estimated at £100,000. See the Gents. Mag. for that year pp.477-531.

Over the fireplace in the library is a picture after *Van Dyke*, of most of K. Charles the First's children, viz. *Charles II., James II., Henry, Duke of Gloucester, as an infant*, who died Sept. 13th, 1660, aged 20, *Mary,* who married William, Prince of Orange, and *Elizabeth,* who died in prison, Sept. 8th, 1650.

BILLIARD ROOM

Six pictures by *Peter Roestrate,* a Dutch painter, who died in London 1698, aged 71, viz. *An Old Man Smoking and his Wife spinning, A couple feasting on Oysters, A Cobbler whistling at his work, A Surgeon coolly dressing the leg of a peasant writhing in pain, A Woman holding a Pluck, a Lady at her Toilette.*

Two noble views of Chudleigh Rock, by *W. Tomkins,* in 1779. Died 1792, aged 62.

Two of Ugbrooke Park, by *Towne* before mentioned.

Over the chimney-piece, *A favourite Dog.*

Anne Clifford, Countess of Dorset and Pembroke, taken in 1670, aged 80. She is placed between her parents, *George,* the 3rd Earl of Cumberland and *Margaret (Russell).*

An Engagement with Banditti.

In the gallery between the library and billiard room, is a portrait of *Hugh,* the 4th Lord Clifford, by *Keenan,* and of the late Lord, by *Pickersgill.*

In the sitting room there are a variety of family portraits; among these the most striking is that of the *Duchess of Norfolk. A Mastiff* wounded by a thorn in his foot, painted by *Schniders* or *Sneyders,* the friend of *Rubens;* also in the Staircase, *Interior of the House of Lords at the passing of the Catholic Emancipation Bill. Ramsey.*

1. Not only did Dr. Clifford as before stated reside at Bramble, but the Colonel also; this old residence has been burnt down.

CHAPTER VII

The entrance of Chudleigh parish from the Ashburton Road is by a bridge over the Teign, about a mile from the town. Stokelake House and grounds belonging to the parish of Hennock claim our notice from their immediate vicinity. Stokelake has frequently changed owners: at the commencement of the present century it was purchased of a Mr. Harper, by the Rev. W.F. Bayley, who built the present house which is a pleasant villa situated on the brow of a hill directly above the bridge, and commands a fine view of the rocks and woods on the opposite side. Stokelake is now the property and residence of A. Chichester, Esquire, one of our county magistrates, who has greatly improved its grounds and adjoining farm. The trees belonging to it form a striking termination to the vale of Chudleigh, which here unfolds itself in a scene of surpassing beauty.

Rocklands, an elegant villa, stands on an eminence opposite the bridge. It was built in 1839 by Captain Kerr and purchased a few years since by Admiral Sir David Dunn; its plantations that skirt the road a considerable way towards Chudleigh are rising into great beauty.

Heightly Cottage lies on the right, embosomed in trees the growth of centuries, among which there is a fine specimen of the cedar of Lebanon. This cottage is surrounded by a garden lawn and commands picturesque views of the rocks and the riding parks which it adjoins. Before the Reformation it was included in the church lands, but after becoming the inheritance of Eastchurch it was called the manor of Heightly, having a residence more ancient than Lawell. This calm and lovely retreat reverts to Lord Clifford on the expiration of the present lease.

Lawell House is situated on the east, about midway between the bridge and the town. In 1722 Sir James Sheppard, sergeant at law, purchased this beautiful domain including the surrounding property, of the executors of James Eastchurch; and the father of the late Lord Clifford, the fourth Baron, purchased the reversion of the same after the death of Frances, widow of James Sheppard, Esquire, in 1768. Lawell House was at one time the most beautiful mansion in the parish. The sash windows were numerous and high, the rooms lofty and convenient. The entrance hall presented an elegant mahogany staircase, and the dining room was a superb apartment. It was approached from the Plymouth Road through a noble avenue of trees. Though desolation has been the fate of Lawell, three or four of these noble elms are still standing as if to mourn over the relic of former greatness. It is now a melancholy object; every effort to deface this once handsome residence has been successfully accomplished. What remains is covered with ivy; when this plant is united with ruins on which time has laid his hand, it not only preserves the tottering fabric, but invests it with a double interest; here on the contrary it gives a desolate and neglected appearance to this once pleasant abode.

Chudleigh Rock, situated in Lawell Park, is the southern extremity[1] of a stratum of mountain limestone for which our neighbourhood has been long celebrated. The quarries are most ancient, their lime enriching its own and neighbouring parishes. The varieties of marble they afford have also been much in request for ornamental purposes. That of Chudleigh Rock is principally black, with large veins of white spar crossing it in different directions, and has also a small golden vein frequently running through it. There is no limestone harder or that burns to a whiter calx. When this rock was united to the palace the verdant and beautiful summit was not disturbed, but of late years the excavations have been immense and so rapidly carried on as to leave a mere shell in comparison to its original bulk. Had not these lime works been abandoned they must have altogether destroyed this magnificent rock or have left it a mere wreck. It is however satisfactory to every lover of nature to know that the more beautiful part of it will be now preserved uninjured, to be still enjoyed. Numerous views of it, and the surrounding scenery, are to be met with in public as well as private collections of paintings. A new house has been recently built on the site of the old lime-kiln, being a sad encroachment on the romantic spot, and decidedly interfering with its native grandeur. This far-famed rock is spoken of by Polwhele as one of the most striking of our island; he also thus graphically describes its romantic dell: *"from the south-east a hollow opens to the view, with a stream rushing impetuously at the bottom of it, here and there checked in its progress by a great quantity of rude stones"*. This hollow we would add is a deep recess or ravine, and evidently appears to have been formed by some fearful convulsion of nature which rent these rocks asunder. The opposite mass is called Black Rock, but instead of frowning on each other, as they are sometimes said to do in the figurative language of poetry,[2] they here repose amid rich verdure, and agree to heighten each others charms as they unfold the treasures of their kindred masses, and guard the entrance to the dell below. From the Plymouth Road, Chudleigh Rock presents a circular form of grey unbroken marble of considerable bulk and elevation, shrubs and variegated foliage hanging from its summit and concealing its base.

This front has an indentation, each part rounded in a tower-like form, and at the first glance conveying the idea of the remains of a grand baronial castle. It is impossible adequately to impart an idea of the many interesting objects belonging to this romantic spot. It must be explored to be rightly appreciated; visited and revisited before its secret nooks, its caverns, its hermit's chair and all its varied attractions become familiar. When on the summit, the landscape on the north takes in Haldon and Chudleigh; that on the west embraces Canonteign, Hennock and Botter; on the south, Haytor towering in the distance. In the more immediate neighbourhood there are villas, verdant meads, the Teign and the Elizabethan mansion of Pitt, with its Saxon tower. A small battery on the point of the rock that overlooks Lawell was erected by James Sheppard, Esq. for the purpose of planting a few pieces of ordnance from which for his amusement he occasionally fired salutes. Before disturbed by the hand of man, the summit of this rock was reached by a continuous sward stretching from the garden of the old Bishop's Palace; this path now winds round the quarry. An opening on the left when entered presents a most lovely view: Black Rock is immediately opposite covered with hanging woods; beneath lies the deep ravine, and at the northern extremity the animating scene of the Palace quarry which has of late been extensively worked. There still remains a considerable portion of the rock unbroken, and dull must be the mind that feels no glow of delight, no rapt enjoyment while wandering on its summit. Around are variety, beauty and extent 'above, the canopy of the heavens, directing the spirit (thus concentrated) from the visible to the invisible'. Beneath is spread a carpet soft and verdant, springing out of and nourished by the once living atoms of nature, commencing with the lichen, then the moss, then the tiny seed dropped by the bird, or wafted by the breeze, adapted to the scanty soil, and when all is matured by nature's unerring process there arise the herb and flowering shrub that adorn each rocky nook and massive ridge with vegetation. And is it for man that these many wonders are displayed? It is, and man alone can 'look from nature up to nature's God'.

"The glories of whose mind
Leave all our soaring thoughts behind."

An old writer quaintly but correctly observes, on the subject of nature's many wonders *"who so gazes through these with the eye of his soul feels the littleness of man in the greatness of all around"*.

The upper part of the grounds belonging to Lawell known as the Riding Parks, lie east of the dell and stretch towards the hamlet of Gappah. These extensive glades are covered with rich pasture and an abundant variety of wild flowers. The hanging woods that surround them on all sides beautifully harmonise with the scenery of Ugbrooke Park, from which they are separated by a terrace-like road, where splendid views of the country towards the south (already described) can be enjoyed, with the addition of Chudleigh Rock situated immediately below. From these glades various paths wind through the copse to the edge of the dell. Black Rock, before named, is a point of pre-eminent beauty and assumes a turret-like form, hanging over the ravine below, from which the deep murmur of the stream steals on the ear. Ridges of rock jutting from beneath the short turf that covers its summit afford seats for the numbers who visit it during the summer months, and who have here the privilege of enjoying one of the most magnificent views in the kingdom.

The Riding Parks terminate at a point called Mount Pleasant where there anciently stood an inn or resting place for travellers and to which tradition has always given a bad character, and related concerning it many absurd tales of horror and superstition. These appear to have had their origin in mysterious deeds of darkness, which received confirmation of their having been perpetrated from the fact that in a fissure belonging to the adjoining Palace quarry there were found some years since several human skeletons. The cavity in which they were deposited was thirty feet below the surface, and to which there could have been no access but from above. Though thus hidden and private, it was doubtless well known to the rangers of these woods, and by them used as a place of concealment. These skeletons were probably those of wayfaring men or sailors on their route to Plymouth, plundered and murdered at the house before mentioned while sleeping in unconscious security.

The deep recess between Chudleigh and Black Rock, with propriety styled a dell, is about a quarter of a mile in length. The scene at the Palace quarry where it commences is highly picturesque and animating; the dell itself is one of the most beautifully secluded and romantic spots belonging to our vale. The thick woods that enclose it on either side extend to its very depth, and are full of attractions, abounding with wild flowers and having many labyrinth-like paths that conduct from one lovely scene to another. Although there are many different ways by which the adventurous can reach the dell, yet the most easy descent is by a path from the copse adjoining the Riding Parks. The stream as it forces its way over the rugged channel forms a cascade not very considerable, unless after heavy rain, but always a pleasing object as seen between the trees foaming and dashing over the huge stones. The graceful branches of the hazel and other trees, as they are flung across the stream, form a striking contrast to the rude moss covered stones that are variously grouped in their narrow channel. As a whole, it sets all description at defiance, especially when the scene is illumined by a meridian sun which gives to it a golden hue that can only be accounted for by the rays of light penetrating the deep recess amongst the trees, reflected by the sparkling and dashing stream. The attractions of the dell may be judged of from the fact that through the months of summer and autumn artists are from day to day employed amid its solitude in endeavouring to portray its striking and peculiar features. The stream that flows through the dell is called Kate Brook; it rises on Haldon, its course is east of the town, receiving in its progress the limpid springs of Waddon.

Above the town it is diverted from its natural channel to work three successive flour mills. Imagination pictures it on entering the dell as revelling in enjoyment at its restoration to liberty; however, it has again to be dammed up by a weir to supply the Chudleigh Bridge Mill when, after crossing the Newton Road, it falls into the Teign.

The Pixies Hole, as it is commonly called, from its being the supposed habitation of a diminutive race of fairies that are said to delight in solitary places such as pathless woods and mountain streams. Dancing in a ring has always been described as their chief amusement, and they are also accused of playing off mischievous tricks on man and beast. The reader may obtain from Mrs. Bray's *'Legends of Devon'* further information concerning these tiny elves, and the opinions entertained of them by the peasantry of our rural districts. We would simply suggest that our Pixies Hole, from its magnitude and importance, may be considered a kind of royal habitation of the Elfin King and his high court of sovereignty. The Chudleigh Cavern is thus noticed by Risdon, *"there is a cave hereabouts which creepeth far under the ground, of which many marvellous matters are spoken"*.

The entrance, almost concealed by trees, is midway down the rock and is reached by a steep and irregular pathway; it is arched and is ten feet high and twelve feet wide, with a passage, the extreme length of which is 135 feet, terminating in a spacious cavity, formed within the bowels of the rock. At the distance of about sixty feet from the entrance an almost abrupt termination seemed till lately to have presented itself, and it was with some difficulty and in a creeping position that the explorer could proceed further. However, this inconvenience no longer exists, the hole being considerably enlarged by the removal of the alluvial soil which lay beneath a thick calcarious incrustation, and the entire length of this natural tunnel can now be traversed in an erect position till the large apartment just named is reached. This is an irregularly shaped space, its length being thirty nine feet, its greatest height about fifty feet, and the breadth twelve feet, not cheered even by a single ray of light. Fragments of rock lie promiscuously scattered about, and great caution must be used in passing between them, and it will be thus seen that lights are absolutely necessary for the exploration of this noble cavern. From this principal cavity another branches off of greater regularity and more vaulted appearance. This second passage is nine feet in breadth, eleven feet in height and seventy two feet in length and is called the Pixies Parlour;[3] the bottom of which is level. On its left at the end of another passage a few rays of light are admitted through a fissure, sufficiently large for an individual to pass with some little difficulty. At the end of the Pixies Parlour, on the right, there is a passage-like fissure about three feet wide, gradually narrowing to about one foot to the length of thirty; further on through this narrow aperture some individuals have passed and reached the opposite side of the rock into the old quarry. This fissure appears to go through the bulk of the rock from side to side as it is quite visible in the northern exterior.

Opposite the entrance, within the principal cavity, by creeping through a narrow archway another large recess presents itself, and there is no doubt from the many fissures that may be seen around that many other subterranean passages of even still greater extent may belong to this rock that the foot of man has never yet trod. In traversing these dreary inroads into an apparently solid rock, on looking up huge pieces of stone naturally suspended overhead seem from their gloomy aspect and ponderous weight to strike the mind with terror, while on the other hand it is somewhat relieved by the fantastic incrustations with which the sides, especially of the large apartment, are covered. One of these depositions demands particular attention as it used, and is now by a few, to some extent, regarded as the guardian idol of the cavern. It is situated on the left at the entrance a few feet above the ground, presenting the rude outline of the human head, and is vulgarly called the 'Pope's Head'. It is soft and porous, being the inorganic deposit of the decomposed rock brought down by the continual droppings that are always traversing through the veins of this natural massive structure. In order to be protected from the tricks which the wicked little inhabitants would play the visitors of this gloomy region, it was formerly deemed absolutely necessary to stick pins into the 'Pope's Head', and even now the custom is not altogether obsolete. Now and then a wag of more temerity than veneration would strip the shrine of its offerings and risk the heavy penalties that might be inflicted by the vengeful and mysterious occupants of this dreary abode.

By the permission of Lord Clifford, Professor Buckland and Mr. Northmore commenced an examination of this cavern on the 12th April, 1825, when in the alluvial soil that was deposited beneath the calcarious incrustation their research was rewarded by a variety of fossil bones,[4] belonging to beasts of prey, similar to those found in Kirkdale and Kents Hole. It was in consequence of these researches that a more convenient entrance was obtained. Dr. Buckland discovered what appeared to him to be a British kitchen, charcoal, pottery, flint knives, &c. Mr. Northmore also found in the interior of the cavern a great quantity of mud, at some parts two or three feet deep, at others he sounded six or eight feet without reaching the bottom. He also discovered what he considered to be an oxide of manganese lying about three or four feet below the surface, and continuing nearly through the whole length of the cavern. These learned gentlemen were highly pleased with their discoveries; however, they differed widely in their geological theories, each considering that his own scientific deductions were illustrated and confirmed by what was here presented.

Here during the summer months parties regale themselves and fires are sometimes lighted; the effect is striking as the flames play about the dark recesses of this gloomy abode. In bringing this sketch of the Pixies Hole to a close, it appears necessary to observe that it cannot be rightly appreciated without being visited. Its awful shades, lengthened caverns, rudely ornamental sides, venerable rocks, woods and dell to which it belongs make it altogether superior to that which we have by dimensions and divisions attempted to describe. Banditti might have chosen it as a proper place to have held their revels and there can be no doubt of its having been used as a resort or hiding place by the Aborigines in times of danger. Though there are no traces whatever of its having been appropriated for religious purposes, yet it might have been thus used as it admirably accorded with the gloomy superstition of the Druids.

On descending into the quarry near where the old lime kiln formerly stood another object well worthy investigation presents itself. It is one of those chasms that are, as well as larger cavities, frequently met with and natural to limestone formations. The one here is altogether different from the Pixies Hole and is of considerable length, about four feet in width and twelve feet in height; the water finds its way from above and, by the process of crystallisation, columns resembling the vaulted aisles of a cathedral cover its sides; these incrustations follow in uniform succession and preserve throughout the most artistic effect. In addition to these richly adorned sides, when first discovered this cavity had transparent alabaster-like stalactites hanging from its pointed roof. These from their brittle nature, and the desire of visitors to possess them, have nearly all disappeared. It seems an established law according to geologists that these stalactites must live and increase by the process of their first formation or else in becoming quiescent and stationary the adhesion ceases and they crumble to powder. The process of crystallisation in this chasm appears to be still going forward.

1. Southern extremity is only used here as a relative term.

2. Even prose, *"the stupendous tors of Dartmoor and Haytor frown on each other with sublime grandeur above the intervening vales."* Moore.

3. A fete was held here on the 27th July, 1840, in honour of the Honourable Mr. Clifford who had attained the age of maturity; the splendid cavern was illuminated by a number of fairy lanterns whose twinkling lights were most enchanting; the interior was also decorated with laurel and oak branches interspersed with choice flowers. The visitors were accommodated with rustic seats and also a plentiful supply of viands and rich delicacies on rustic tables erected for the purpose. A Glee of Lord Mornington's was sung, *"Here in cool grot and mossy cell, where rural Fays and Fairies dwell"*. On the fairy shades being instantaneously removed from the lanterns a bright blaze of splendid light shone forth illuminating every dark recess. The numerous visitors were purposely intercepted and conducted to the fairy cave by an individual attired in green with artificial wings representing 'Ariel', the leading character of the enchanting scene.

4. Fossil bones of mammiferous animals are still found under the stalagmitic floors of these caverns and, indeed, in many caverns in the limestone ranges of South Devon.

CHAPTER VIII

The north-east division of this parish, to which we now invite the reader's attention, is fraught with interest from its having been occupied by some of the most ancient and influential families of the neighbourhood; it is also distinguished for many natural advantages and rural beauty. To its ancient names of Harcombe, Waddon and Hams, many others of more modern origin have been added. The Teignmouth Road divides it from the Ugbrooke Vale, and on the west it is bounded by the highway to Plymouth. It is completely sheltered from the north and east winds by Haldon, which rises immediately above, and is a tract of land of considerable extent, whose varied features are somewhat difficult to describe. In addition to the stratum of mountain lime rock that traverses it from Chudleigh to Haldon, there are massive ridges of considerable elevation that rise towards the west. The smaller fragments of rocks are scattered in endless variety in the background, some clothed with ivy and various plants, others altogether bare, while others again sink beneath the verdant sod. These rocky heights are planted with apple trees whose growth is not so large as those in the clay soils but they bear plentifully. The air of this upland region is dry and elastic, yet genial. Springs of water clear as crystal are here abundant, welling up beneath the lime rocks, irrigating the meadows that stretch towards the vale and supplying the farms and cottages on their way.

We now proceed to particularise a few of the most interesting localities. Hams Barton first claims our attention, which is soon reached by crossing Kate Brook and then proceeding either by road or path fields. The house is inclosed in a court and is marked by a few chestnut trees. It is thus noticed by Polwhele, *"Hams was formerly the seat of the family of Hunt, situated about three quarters of a mile from Chudleigh". "In this parish"*, says Risdon *"Hunt have their habitation where they have inheritances."* Hams was an estate of very considerable extent when in possession of the Hunts. It afterwards belonged to the Ingletts, now the Fortescue family, of whom what remained was bought by one Beech, who sold it to Sir Robert Palk, and it was finally purchased by Lord Clifford. A portion only of the old mansion is standing; what remains is in good repair and occupied as a farm. Its style is early gothic; the principal doorway with several others are granite arched, the door itself massive and altogether antique, the ceilings of some of the rooms are unplastered, being of oak exactly smoothed and jointed, as was common with these ancient residences. The windows anciently were of stained glass, but have been displaced for others or blocked up, and now some of them are modern sash windows. To the old house an addition was made of a servants hall and a banqueting room in 1621. It has a vaulted ceiling enriched in compartments rising above a deep cornice. The arms of Hunt are over the chimney-piece,[1] and the royal arms at the upper end of the room; these were formerly no doubt emblazoned and painted. The decorations are in a good state of preservation, but disfigured by whitewash. The pedigree of this family is traced by the Herald's Visitation, to 1620 they are mentioned as belonging to Exeter and Chudleigh; Thomas Hunt was Mayor of Exeter in 1517 and another of the same name in 1537. There are various entries in the parish register of this family from 1564 to 1730 when the last entry was made.

Upcott is situated north-east, not far from Hams Barton, with it the rocky district commences; the farmhouse was built by the Rev. G. Burrington (father of the late vicar) about a century ago. It commands fine views towards the south and is sheltered by the lime rocks. Upcott cannot but be regarded with deep interest when it is known to be the birthplace of Major James Rennell, whose family classed with the respectable yeomanry of the neighbourhood. Their ancient inheritance still stands and is known as Rennell's farm, which is situated at Waddon a short distance from Upcott, and to which place the parents of the Major must have removed not long before his birth. The name of Rennell is of frequent occurrence in the parish register, also amongst 'the seven men': talents of no ordinary kind was the birthright of this ancient family. The descendants from another branch who resided at Fishwick, in the parish of Kingsteignton, were distinguished even to a late date by superior taste in sculpture and painting; belonging to the Chudleigh Rennells we would direct attention not only to Major James but also to Thomas who was born in 1718. He was a painter of considerable merit; his works (amongst many others) gained him the patronage of the Duke and Duchess of Kingston;[2] but every favour and advantage conferred on him was wholly lost by his indolence and improvidence. His scientific knowledge and inventive powers were considerable; he was an excellent chemist for that day, preparing his own colours, and is said to have acquired the art of fixing the most fading. Many of his early productions were in the town before the fire; two or three are still in existence. He is said to have excelled in the drapery of his portraits. He resided many years at Plymouth, and from thence removed to Dartmouth, where he lived in great poverty; however, about two years before his death he enjoyed a comfortable home through the bounty of J. Seale, Esquire. His death took place October 19th, 1788.

Major James Rennell was born 1742 at Upcott in this parish, and at an early age attended a writing school at Chudleigh. It is probable that the wonders of the then busy town, contrasting with the quiet of his rural home, elicited his genius and aroused his power of close observation and exact delineation which raised him to the greatest eminence. At an early age he took a map of the town which was a performance of sufficient merit to attract the attention of the Rev. Gilbert Burrington, through whose interest he was made a midshipman at the age of fifteen; he quitted it for the army when about twenty-four and was sent on active service to India where he soon distinguished himself by his various charts of the Indian coast and his observations on the bank and current of Cape Lagullas. He may be said to have commenced altogether a new era in geography and is considered as the first cosmographer of his own or indeed of any age, his discoveries being most valuable to the navigator, and the world at large. His laborious researches were not confined to modern geography alone, for his treatises &c. are now the highest authorities to which the classical student can appeal.[3] His kindness and integrity were also bright accompaniments to his superior talents. The valuable assistance he rendered Mungo Park, in preparing his travels in Africa for publication, made it one of the most interesting and popular works of its day. He died on the 29th March, 1830, universally respected and regretted; his remains were interred in Westminster Abbey. The name of Rennell was lost to the parish with the parents of Major James; the Fishwick branch in the male line is also extinct.

Upcott just mentioned, may be considered to occupy a central position amidst the surrounding lime rocks, and its quarry has been extensively worked; in the centre of its rock there are imbedded in sand marine fossil shells of perfect form, and classed by Professor Phillips as *"Murchisonia Spinosa"*.

The ancient Waddene Rock and its immediate vicinity are now known by the more inelegant name of Porcombe. The rock is situated in a copse adjoining Upcott and the extensive excavations that have been here carried on have left only a broken ridge of some length, plainly indicating that it was once the most magnificent development of mountain lime rock in the parish. In connection with this quarry stood the ancient 'Waddene' hamlet, the ruins of which were well known to some of the old inhabitants of the neighbourhood, and were taken down by the late Lord Clifford in consequence of their being a haunt for vagrants and smugglers. By a straight path through the copse the old quarry is soon reached, and it presents a scene of rural beauty and unusual stillness where all was once bustle and activity. The old lime kiln is deep and cavernous, shrouded with various plants, while a tree of some size grows from its very centre. Amongst many other trees that surround and adorn this favoured spot there are two large beeches which are splendid specimens of the order to which they belong; their extended branches and close foliage, so peculiar to their growth and the position they occupy, strikingly contrast with the clustered underwood that here and there intersperse and adorn the verdant undulations around. The extensive recesses formed by excavators have altogether lost their rocky character, except where the rude outline of the broken ridge rises above the tangled wreaths woven by the spontaneous operations of nature. Every hallow and every crevice is covered with vegetation – ivy, clematis, wild rose, underwood and the trailing bramble all here revel in uninterrupted but graceful luxuriance. Fragments of rock that form hillocks around the kiln-head are covered with thyme, lotus and a variety of wild flowers, and it appears as if nature had hastened to hide and repair the shattered remains of its former grandeur by clothing it with extra beauty and fertility. However, the southern aspect, the warm recesses and light soil so peculiar to limestone deposits are the attractions for the early and fragrant violet and all the lovely flowers that adorn the remains of the ancient 'Waddene Rock'.

Modern Waddon (being a port of the ancient district) is about a quarter of a mile south-east of Porcombe; it is an estate of some extent with a respectable farmhouse and several cottages, also a rock but of far less beauty than those towards the west. This estate was evidently at one period divided between the Rennells and the Hellyers; the name of the latter, although not before mentioned, is of frequent occurrence in the parish register and amongst 'the seven men'; the representatives of this family were in succession baptised Christopher. Mr. Hellyer, the last of that name, sold an extensive inheritance at Waddon to the late Lord Clifford. There is a gravestone in the church to the memory of several individuals of this ancient family.

On the west of the rocky district already described is situated Kerswell, purchased a few years since of Sir Lawrence Palk, by Mr. Richards: since it has been in his possession he has greatly improved the surrounding neighbourhood by making a new road from Kerswell to Haldon, and also by building on it a neat and commodious house that commands fine views towards the south, and is adorned with gardens, shrubberies and plantations. Kerswell Rock is one of the most conspicuous of the western ridges and, having an easy access, it is frequently visited by parties during the summer months. The scenery from its summit is remarkably fine and extensive, exciting general admiration. It has in its own neighbourhood the attraction of kindred quarries, a romantic old warren and woody dell. Several farms and villas enliven the scene, but towards Chudleigh the eye is especially attracted, where its rocks and deep ravine are displayed to advantage: while beyond the vale and Knighton Heath the striking objects of many different parishes may be distinctly traced, backed by the wild downs and tors of Dartmoor. The morning mists and summer haze that are frequently seen hanging above the valley, which are the admiration of landscape painters, here especially charm the beholder; indeed none but an artist can rightly appreciate the exquisite loveliness of this extensive view.

It appears here necessary to observe that though Lord Clifford possesses nearly the whole of the Waddon district, still there is on the north an estate of some extent belonging to J.H. Ley, Esquire, known as Higher Upcott.

Harcombe is situated about three miles north-east of Chudleigh. It is here that the ancient families of Stawell and Balle had inheritances. From the pedigree of the Stawells it is seen that the last of the family who belonged to this parish was baptised in 1578, from whom Sir John Stawell of Bovey Tracey was a descendant, although born at Bickington.

The Balles of Higher Harcombe were among the most wealthy and influential of the ancient families of the parish and from them the Mamhead branch (so well known in the history of the county) descended. On the side of the glen, immediately opposite their old heritage at Harcombe, a mansion was began to be built by the last of the Balles; this accidentally took fire which not only stopped the progress of the building, but caused the design of its erection to be altogether relinquished. Some of the old walls are still standing; such of the materials as were worth removing were taken to Mamhead to form part of a mansion there. It is well known that Thomas Balle purchased the manor of Ashcombe of Edward Blount, Esquire. No entry occurs in the parish register of the Harcombe Balles later than 1673, but in Ashcombe churchyard there are many gravestones to the memory of Balles, yeomen, and Balles of Mamhead, from 1693 to 1755.

The estate of Higher Harcombe was included in the purchase of Mamhead, and Lower Harcombe was bought by Sir Robert Newman and Mr. Parker, of the executors of the Rev. J. Templer of Lindridge.

Higher Harcombe is now a farm of considerable extent, adjoining and comprising a portion of Haldon; it was considered one of the poorest farms in the neighbourhood, having been greatly neglected for a long time. However, about seven years ago T. Newman, Esquire considered that the tract of land was a good field for the introduction of the modern system of agriculture. Accordingly a most substantial and convenient farmhouse was erected and from that period to the present, under the management of his Bailiff and the direct superintendence of himself, a thorough system of draining has been carried on, coupled with the application of the practical improvements which of late years science has pointed out (this of course has been attended with a considerable outlay of capital), but as may be expected the value of the farm is enhanced tenfold and we have now, instead of the almost waste piece of land, a first-rate model farm in a high state of cultivation, producing its average crops and taking completely the lead of its neighbours. This tract of land resembles in cultivation and scenery the well known glens of Scotland.

The population of the hamlet of Harcombe comprises about 60; the cottages are detached and solitary, from being united to a glen that belongs to Haldon, and the character of its scenery differs essentially from the vale of Chudleigh. It is pleasing to add that private benevolence has provided for the children of Harcombe a week and Sabbath school, and the aged have also the privilege of enjoying a cottage service on the Sabbath. Generous Christian sympathy can never be more beneficially employed than when engaged in promoting the spiritual welfare, and in providing for the wants of these remote rural districts.

Whiteway lies about two and a half miles north of Chudleigh at the foot of Haldon. It was the ancient inheritance of the Bennetts;[4] their pedigree is given by Westcott who states that Richard Bennett married Julyan, the daughter of William Whiteway of Chudleigh. It is now the seat of M.E.N. Parker, Esquire, [5] formerly member for the southern division of the county, and who was High Sheriff for Devon in 1850. The present mansion stands on the site of the old residence and is a handsome brick house consisting of a centre and two wings; one only of these was built when the house was erected by Lord Boringdon whose property it was, and who exchanged it for some lands belonging to his younger brother, Montague. Whiteway afterwards passed into the hands of the late Mr. Parker, who added the other wing in 1813, and made every necessary improvement to constitute it a neat, elegant and commodious residence. The entrance to Whiteway is by a lodge gate from the old Exeter Road, and the house is reached in about half a mile's distance by a pleasant drive through an extensive lawn that commands fine views of the vales of Chudleigh and the Teign, with a wide expanse of country beyond. Mr. Parker has considerably added to his estate by recent purchases and has introduced the modern improvements of the day in agriculture. This high state of cultivation and the extensive plantations have entirely altered and greatly improved the aspect of this neighbourhood. Oxencombe, belonging to this estate situated east of Whiteway, is one of the largest farms in the parish, having on it several lime kilns. The extensive preserves belonging to Whiteway are well stocked with game.

Filleigh, the residence and property of Major Milles, is situated about a mile from the town and the open and extensive lawn in which the house stands is a gentle eminence, lying on the western side of the vale. There is belonging to it two entrances, one from the old and the other from the new Exeter Road; these roads bound the estate on either side. Filleigh House faces the east but is sheltered on the north by a thick copse or woods, and beyond, there belongs to its fine plantations of firs. While it enjoys pleasant views, it is itself a great addition to the scenery as beheld on the other side of the vale, or from the road that skirts it.

Oaklands, the residence of T. Lane, Esquire, was built by Major

Milles on some coarse clay land called Filleigh Farm, situated west of the old Exeter Road. The reader who a few years since might have known this sterile tract of land, the worst in the parish with the exception of Haldon, would now scarcely recognise it. This great change has been effected by a judicious and experimental system of farming under the direct superintendence of the occupier, who has literally converted this once barren waste into fruitful fields, bearing average crops. On returning from Filleigh Farm to the new Exeter Road there remain to be noticed Oakfield House, Heathfield Cottage and Littlehill House. These modern residences are adorned with fine trees of ancient growth, their gardens and shrubberies being kept in excellent order, and well contrast with the rich variety and luxuriance of the opposite district of Waddon.

Before leaving this locality it will be necessary to notice Culver House, the present residence of T. Yarde, Esquire, which within the last two years has been considerably enlarged. The gardens have been newly arranged and greatly improved, and to them has been added a beautiful conservatory.

The Yarde family[6] is amongst the most ancient in the county and, as a direct descendant, Mr. T. Yarde has lately come into the possession of the family estate of Whiteway in the parish of Kingsteignton. The town must feel greatly indebted to him for his many improvements and a considerable outlay of capital.

It would only weary the reader's attention to enumerate the different estates belonging to the western division of the parish as they present no distinct features or peculiarities; as a whole they may be described as well wooded with extensive orchards and scenery highly picturesque, the whole tract consisting of an alternation of hill and dale, with the exception of some fine marshes that adjoin the Teign. This river is reached by many romantic roads across the hills that wind by steep descents, or through the verdant meadows of Northwood. Having already traced the sinuous course of the Teign from its granite embedded fountain head on Dartmoor (the birthplace of Devonshire rivers) to its joining the sea at Teignmouth, we must now notice the fish for which this river is remarkable; it contains salmon, peel, grilse, sea trout or truff, gravelling and heppers, all of the species of salmo; trout and eel are also plentiful. It was lately thought necessary to protect the fish; accordingly about four years since the 'Teignbridge Fishing Association' was formed, which now consists of upwards of seventy members of the most wealthy and influential of the neighbourhood and elsewhere; the fishing for the last few years has been seriously injured by the mineral waters of the mines near Ashton flowing into it, and the destruction of the fish has at times been very great: the society has however remedied the evil by a scientific arrangement of catch pits which collect and allow the deleterious matter held in suspension to precipitate, previous to its influx into the river, and the result is that the Teign abounds with fish and is the favourite resort of numberless sportsmen who delight in the capture of its finny inhabitants.

It remains for us to add that the Teign near Crocombe is a most beautiful clear stream murmuring over a rough and shallow bed and at some places altogether concealed by trees. The bridge here may be considered a central point from which many different parishes can be reached. The hills on the western side rise to a considerable height, their rocky summits surmounting the woods present a striking appearance, the vallies are interspersed with several farms, and the woods sweep along the banks of the river as far as Chudleigh Bridge.

Before concluding this brief sketch of the scenery of Chudleigh it will be necessary to offer a few remarks on Haldon, which in part belongs to the parish, and forms the entire of its north and north-east boundary. It is traversed by many roads along which can be enjoyed the fine views and fresh breezes from the English Channel, together with the rich valley of Exminster and Exeter in the distance. Haldon presents to the antiquarian and geologist many interesting features in ancient camps, barrows and roads, fossils and a variety of sands and coloured earths, while the flints themselves if selected are a valuable ingredient in the manufacture of porcelain and china, as well as for repairing roads. Amongst many fertile and lovely eminences that environ Haldon, one only claims our attention from its being the most thickly wooded grove in the neighbourhood: it is styled Box Hill and lies above the Dunscombe vale east of Chudleigh, forming a wood crowned height to Ugbrooke Park; while it is worthy notice that in one of the largest fields of the parish and adjoining this plantation the park and its richly clad eminences forcibly present themselves. The buildings and other animating features that are enjoyed when within its precincts being altogether hid, and the whole landscape is well backed up by the deep blue hills towards the South Hams.

Geology is not like scenery confined to a certain locality, nor are its indications often visible on the surface. It is a science requiring deep research and a wider range than Devonshire or even England afford. The following observations with which the writer has been favoured will, it is trusted, prove interesting and instructive.

"The geological structure of the parish of Chudleigh belongs to the great Devonian formation, consisting of slate covered occasionally with trappean ash, locally called dunstone, which occupy a position somewhere intermediate between the silurian strata of Wales and the old red sandstone of other countries. It contains from three to four hundred fossils peculiar to itself, with drifted fragments of trilobites, and other remains belonging to an earlier period: it is traversed by several veins of limestone, formerly coral reefs, made up to a great

extent of zoophital remains which commonly go under the name of madrepores; near Chudleigh as in other parts of the county, the limestone forms a serviceable marble. The faces of the rocks exhibit the most unequivocal marks of the sea at one time having dashed against them; and the neighbouring deep ravine would seem to have been scooped out by an oceanic current. After this a bed of marine alluvial matter must have been deposited in the ravine, remains of which may still be seen near to where the brook enters. By the erosive action of this brook its channel has sunk down in the alluvial bed in some places to a depth of forty or fifty feet. The occurrence of scattered and partially water-worn stones, the same as those we now find in the channel of the brook, would seem to indicate that the stream must formerly have flowed at a much higher level. The whole of the valley to the south-west, extending from Bovey to Newton, must at one time have been covered by the sea which did not entirely take its departure till within the historical period, as anchors have been found in the Bovey coalfield. That the clay and grit of this field must have been deposited by the sea there can be little doubt; it is also equally obvious that the trees and vegetable matter must have been washed down from the surrounding hills by tides and currents. But where such an immense thickness of wood as that which is now undergoing compression into coal could have been drifted from it is very difficult to understand. We have evidence of the whole of Devon, including Dartmoor, having, at a much earlier period, been covered by the sea. The drifted fragments of rock found scattered along the south-western declivities of Dartmoor can only be explained by reference to the action of oceanic currents; while in the district of Chudleigh there are boulder stones which would seem to indicate a similar agency, if not, perhaps the action of floating ice."

Words however well chosen can never convey just ideas of scenery and it must be admitted that after every effort on the writer's part the many attractions of this locality have been but faintly portrayed, and in order to appreciate the rich and harmonious grandeur that nature has so bountifully bestowed on this favoured spot, the neighbourhood itself must be visited.

1. Az., on a bend between two water bougets, or., three leopards faces, gules. Crest. On a mount, V., a hound seiant, or., collared, G., chained to a pikestaff, S., the head per pale, or. and argent.
2. The Duchess of Kingston, as it is perhaps well known, was the beautiful Miss Chudleigh of Ashton. A town in Russia named Chudleigh was called after her as the writer has been informed.
3. He published illustrations of the *"Expedition of the younger Cyrus and the retreat of the ten thousand Greeks"*, *"Observations on the topography of the Plain of Troy"*, also on the *"Topography of Ancient Babylon"*.
4. Arms. Sable, a chevron erminois between three tripled ears of wheat, or.
5. Arms. Sable, a stag's head caboshed between two flaunches, Arg.
6. Arms. Argent, a chevron, gules, between three water bougets, sable.

APPENDIX

The winter of 1813-14 was very severe throughout Europe, particularly so in England. In January 1814 the most extraordinary fall of snow occurred in the west of England that had been known in the memory of man; and after several years nothing similar has happened. The following extracts from a Naturalist's Calendar kept at the time at Chudleigh may prove interesting in reference to such an unusual phenomenon.

J.P.J.

JANUARY 1814

1st.   A fine mild day. The sun shone out quite warm, the moles are throwing up their heaps in the fields in great quantities; this is generally considered to be a sign of rain.

"And feel at every step,
Our foot half sunk in hillocks green and soft,
Rais'd by the mole, the miner of the soil."

A clear unclouded night, Poa Annua (*annual meadow grass*), Lamium Purpureum (*Red Dead Nettle*), Leontodon Taraxacum (*Dandelion*), Bellis Perennis (*common Daisy*), Senecio Vulgaris (*common Groundsel*). Fl.

2nd.   Thick fog in the morning – fine day – cloudy evening.

3rd.   Heavy fall of rain.

4th.   Cold dreary day – occasional falls of snow.

5th.   Severe frost, and heavy fall of snow several inches deep – birds congregate.

6th.   Heavy fall of snow in the morning – fine day – severe frost in the evening and very cold.

7th.   Cold north wind – cloudy – severe frost – the snow covers the ground.

8th. Frost – fine clear day – the birds are become tame.

9th. Frost – fine clear day.

10th. Very severe frost – pools frozen over – wind east.

11th. During the last night and the greater part of today the snow fell in great quantities, the wind blew very strong to the north and north-east, and drifted the snow at some places to the height of six and eight feet. Such a fall of snow was never remembered by the oldest person; it beat with such violence that it was almost impossible to leave the house, all travelling was stopped. The mail coach was several times overturned; none of the other coaches attempted to proceed; the march of a regiment of soldiers was prevented; some houses could hardly be approached, all the entrances being blocked up with snow. It was certainly the most surprising snowstorm ever experienced in this part of the country. It ceased snowing about 4 o'clock p.m., when the wind subsided, but the heavens continued very gloomy, and a little snow fell about 9 o'clock p.m.; the cold was not very intense.

12th. A fine clear day but very cold – severe frost – the River Teign frozen over – the snow deep in the roads, no carriages able to pass – the mails carried on horseback – birds feed on the vegetables in the gardens and numbers of them found dead.

> *How find the myriads that in summer cheer*
> *The hills and vallies with their ceaseless songs*
> *Due sustenance, or where subsist they now.*
> *Earth yields them nought; the imprisoned worm is safe*
> *Beneath the frozen clod; all seeds of herbs*
> *Lie covered close; and berry bearing thorns*
> *That feed the thrush (whatever some suppose)*

Afford the smaller minstrels no supply.
The long protracted rigour of the year
Thins all their num'rous flocks. In chinks and holes
Ten thousand seek an unmolested end
As instinct prompts, self-buried ere they die.

13th.   Fine day but severely cold – carriages are drawn through the snow with great difficulty – the mail from London did not arrive until 7 o'clock p.m., 18 hours later than the usual time.

14th.   The day was ushered in with a strong east wind and piercing cold – at 9 o'clock a.m. the snow began to fall, and continued for several hours. All the attempts which had been made to render the roads passable became useless, as the drifting of the snow again blocked up the roads. Several who attempted to pass over Haldon and in various other directions were obliged to return to the town. The coach came from Plymouth but could not proceed any further. The heaps of snow at some places reached to the roofs of the houses.

15th. It thawed a little – cloudy and a thick fog. I walked about a mile from the town on the Exeter Road to see a pass cut in the snow; before this was effected all travelling was stopped; snow completely filled up the road and was from eight to twelve feet in height. A sight so very unusual attracted many spectators; the roads having been cleared carts passed and the mails were carried on horseback.

16th. Thaw during the day, and thick fog, a great many people who were detained by the snow were able to leave the town – the coaches could not proceed the whole way from Plymouth to Exeter – the snow is disappearing very gradually without rain – a fortunate circumstance as danger was apprehended from floods.

117

17th. Snow disappearing gradually – a number of travellers who had been detained passed today – it froze towards the evening, and about 8 o'clock p.m. snow began again to fall.

18th. Snow and rain.

19th. Snow with sleet and rain – the melting of the snow has again rendered the roads impassable – the coaches were forced to return to the town, being unable to pass over Haldon. A heavy fall of snow in the evening.

20th. A great drift of snow during the night and severe frost – all travelling prevented – the coach passengers detained in the town – the streets filled with large heaps of snow.

21st. Severe frost – fine day – fall of snow in the evening – the unusual severity of the weather continues in full force – the coaches and wagons are buried in the snow on Haldon. In some of the streets steps are cut in the snow to descent to the houses.

22nd. Severe frost – cold day, and occasional falls of snow – a number of people passed on horseback, the only mode of travelling.

23rd. Severe frost and cold north wind.

24th. Frost – a number of labourers working on the turnpike roads.

25th. Frost, but the wind not quite so cold. The roads however cleared of the snow and many carriages passed. The mails still come in at irregular hours.

26th. Rapid thaw with rain and thick fog towards the evening. The general average depth of the snow has been about three feet. A great number of birds have died and the hares entered the gardens near the town for the vegetables, and got entangled in the snow.

27th. Thick frost during the night – thaw with rain.

28th. Thaw – fine day – the sun shone out warm – the ground appears at some places – the snow in the streets disappearing gradually – the snow was drifted to the height of 18 and 20 feet at some places.

29th. Thaw – in the morning the wind was south – about noon it came round to the north-west, and blew a tremendous storm, and a little snow fell – the report that some soldiers were lost in the snow on Haldon is incorrect; a single life has not been lost anywhere. The barometer fell to 30*p*. below 28*in*.

30th. Fine day – cold and frosty towards the evening – the Teign has overflowed its banks.

31st. Cold dreary day – falls of snow and hail.

FEBRUARY

1st.   Slight frost and cold north wind.

2nd. Cold gloomy day – rain – the snow rapidly melting away.

3rd.   Severe white frost and cold cloudy day.

4th.   Fine day – the snow gradually disappearing without a flood.

5th.   Rain and sleet.

6th.   Cloudy – rain – violent east wind.

7th.   Stormy – occasional storms and thick fog in the evening.

8th.   Violent east wind – showers – a rainbow appeared – the snow has almost disappeared, except a little which has drifted under the hedges.

FINIS

Chudleigh Parish Councillors
2003—2007

Mr. W. Stanyon, Chairman
Mr. D. Bone, Vice Chairman
Mrs. W. Bishop
Mr. G. Day
Mrs. L. Evans
Mr. S Evans
Mr. D. Laing
Mr. M. Moyse
Mr. R. Smith
Mr. M. Tulley
Mr. C. Webb
Mr. C. West
Mrs. P. Wills

Clerk: Mr. P. Vogel